EMPOWERING CHILDREN

Dr. Jayakaran's passion for the principles of child participation is deeply rooted in a biblical view of children. This view allows him to celebrate and affirm the worth and respect for every child's voice—from the most educated to the most marginalized and exploited. This is a must-read for anyone desiring a strong link to the children with whom they minister.

—Phyllis Kilbourn, Ph.D.
Founder and International Director
Crisis Care Training International

If you or your organization works with children, you need to have this book and make its contents your own. This book helps us take the voice and dreams of children seriously as key contributions to the transformational development process. This book is practical and useful, full of simple exercises that can be used to empower children and allow their voices to be heard and understood. This book is written for practitioners, people living on the front lines of ministry, who need simple tools and the instructions to begin using them the next day. Agencies concerned for child-focused transformational development and children at risk owe Ravi Jayakaran a vote of thanks.

—Bryant L. Myers, Ph.D.
Professor of International Development
School of Intercultural Studies
Fuller Theological Seminary

Empowering Children is the culmination of more than two decades of field-based learning. Dr. Jayakaran combines accounts of personal experiences in the field, listening and learning with children and their families, with practical guidance and tools for the aspiring child participation practitioner. This book will be an invaluable tool for all those committed to involving children meaningfully in the development process.

—Paul Stephenson, M.S.
Director, Child Development and Rights
World Vision International

PRINCIPLES, STRATEGIES, AND TECHNIQUES
FOR MOBILIZING CHILD PARTICIPATION
IN THE DEVELOPMENT PROCESS

EMPOWERING CHILDREN

Ravi Jayakaran

with Jennifer Orona

WILLIAM CAREY
LIBRARY

Naomi Bradley-McSwain, copyeditor
Hugh Pindur, graphic design
Rose Lee-Norman, indexer

Photographs contributed by:
Andrew Lok, Noel Lo, and Mariana Chan (World Vision, China)
Kotaro Ichikawa and team (Foundation for International Development/Relief, Japan)
Ko Sein Lein, Ko Aung Naing, Ma Tha Nwai Law, and Naomi San (World Vision, Myanmar)
Chea Pyden (Vulnerable Children Assistance Organization, Cambodia)
Mom Thany (Child Rights Foundation, Cambodia)
Sabastien Marot (Friends International, Southeast Asia)
The author took other photographs during field visits in various provinces of Cambodia and various countries around the world.

Published by William Carey Library, an imprint of William Carey Publishing
10 W. Dry Creek Circle
Littleton, CO 80120 | www.missionbooks.org

William Carey Library is a ministry of Frontier Ventures
Pasadena, CA 91104 | www.frontierventures.org

Library of Congress Cataloging-in-Publication Data

Jayakaran, Ravi.
Empowering children : principles, strategies, and techniques for
mobilizing child participation in the development process / by Dr. Ravi
Jayakaran, with Jennifer Orona.
p. cm.
Includes bibliographical references.
ISBN 978-0-87808-001-4
1. Youth in development. 2. Young volunteers in community development.
I. Orona, Jennifer. II. Title.
23 22 21 20 19 Printed for Worldwide Distribution

* * *

Dedication

I dedicate this book to my best friend and life partner,

Vimla, who is brilliant with children

and one of the best facilitators I know,

and to children around the world . . .

I hope that we will be able to capture your dreams and aspirations

and understand your fears and apprehensions

as we involve you in the development process.

CONTENTS

* * *

Foreword

I WANT TO remind you of two ideas you already know to be true, and then link them for you. Walk with me here . . .

The first thought is it is so much easier to turn a moving car.

When a car stands still with its hand brake, it can take several strong people to lift it, and then only with great exertion. Conversely, when the engine is humming and you are zipping down the road, most people can turn the wheel with but a single finger.

The same applies to human beings and their development: *When people want to move, they get places.*

The second thought is the notion that humans have no souls. Many scholars have tried to make us believe that we are only intelligent animals, but as followers of Christ, we realize that this is untrue.

We all instinctively know that we do what we do because we believe it is important, that our action is the result of our attitudes, and that our behavior stems from our beliefs.

Now link these two thoughts . . .

Development starts with children. Yet, to help them develop, to get them moving, we need them to participate! It is like moving cars. If we can switch on a child's internal engine, put some fuel in their tank and give them a horizon to travel to, they will get there faster than we could ever drag or carry them.

That fuel is their attitudes and beliefs. The Bible instructs us to "train children in the right way" (Prov. 22:6, NRSV). Child participation is not some new liberation movement, it is wisdom rediscovered. It is good pedagogy. The Bible further instructs us, "Keep your heart with all vigilance, for from it flow the springs of life" (Prov. 4:23, NRSV). We need those young hearts to know how immensely valuable they are, how much they have to contribute, and how eager we are to listen to and understand what children have to say.

If we learn what Ravi is trying to teach us, we could have a very different world to live in and very different children around us—children who know their worth, who do not question their contribution, and who for that reason embrace their obligations to live well and right and grow "in wisdom and in years, and in divine and human favor" (Luke 2:52, NRSV).

Let us grown-ups do our part, so children can do their part. Start now by picking up your pen and this book; read it, mark it, and then *go do it*.

Patrick McDonald
Chief Executive, Viva

* * *

ACKNOWLEDGMENTS

THIS IS ONE book that has taken an exceptionally long time to write. The ultimate completion of the book has been possible because of the efforts and support of many people. I want to especially acknowledge the interactions and contributions of the following people:

Thomas Chan, Bryant Myers, Elsa Lam, Andrew Lok, Jonathan Su, Noel Lo, Mariana Chan, Romaneya, Chea Pyden and team; Mom Thany and team; my former colleagues Manoshi Mitra and Janmejay Singh from the Asian Development Bank; Has Bunton and Uy Bossadine from National Institute of Statistics, Cambodia; Le Xuan Ba, Tran Kim Chung, N.X. Nam, and Phai Le Minh from Central Institute for Economic Management in Hanoi; Chalongphob Sussangkarn, Yongyuth Chalawong and Srawooth Paitoonpong from Thailand Development Research Institute; Chompunch Ramanvongse from the National Economic and Social Development Board of Thailand; Sirivanh Khonethapane, Syviengxay Oraboune, Sithiruth Rasphone and Poh Kong of the National Economic Research Institute of Lao PDR; Nguyen Thi Thu Hien of the Ministry of Planning and Investment in Vietnam; Thida, Esther Pastores, Kotaro Ichikawa, Keiko Maeda, Sebastien Marot, André, Kosal and the Friends International team in Siem Reap; Kyi Minn and his team from World Vision, Myanamar; Oum Sopheap of KHANA (Khemer HIV/AIDS National Alliance), Cambodia; Madame Sunran, Kuntharith, Am Sobol and the team at the Ministry of Education, Youth, and Sport in Cambodia; and Patrick Duong of the United Nations Development Programme, Cambodia.

My work in Asia with international NGOs, The Mekong Institute, the Asian Development Bank, and the UNDP have shown me that field practitioners require techniques that are simple to use, adaptable, and versatile. I am grateful for the things that I learned while working in these contexts, and for my colleagues in each organization.

A special word of thanks also to Patrick McDonald, chief executive of Viva, for his encouragement and support as I wrote this book, and to Paul

Stephenson, Glenn Miles, Joni Middleton, Philippa Lei, Daphne Hollinger, and several others for being willing to read through the draft of the book as peer reviewers in order to give me their valuable feedback and advice for the book to be as effective as possible.

I am grateful to my colleagues at MAP International, especially for the support of Michael Nyenhuis, Mick Smith, and others with IMR, HARO, MAP fellows, and the MAP International country offices—who, though they joined this journey after I completed the book, are all very much on the same journey. Also, to Stephanie Davis, my colleagues from International Justice Mission, and others in Fulton County in Atlanta who work in the fight against the sexual exploitation of children, I extend my thanks.

And last, but not least a special word of thanks to Jennifer Orona, the Viva Equip resources editor, for her hard work in editing this text for consistency and holding me accountable for explaining acronyms and concepts that I had written down presuming everyone understands them. Thanks, Jennifer, for helping this book make it through the final lap to the finish line!

* * *

INTRODUCTION

SEVERAL GLOBAL ORGANIZATIONS have made it their mandate to be *child-focused* in their development approach. This seems to be reasonable and strategic because the child essentially represents the future of the community that one chooses to work in. *The child is the future in the present!* This does not in any way undermine the fact that they are also the present in the present! Even so, focusing on the child is like investing in the future, and ensuring long-term sustainability is the goal.

In 1996, while attending the Global Forum for Child Survival in Atlanta,[1] I had an interesting discussion with several senior representatives from the World Bank, the World Health Organization, and other international organizations. The trend of the discussion was that the economic consequences of failing to provide children with a basic protective safety net could have major global consequences of an economic nature. These were serious enough for some of those not normally involved in development to take a serious look at involvement at an early stage of the child's life. In essence, this means that the child has to be brought into the focus of all development considerations, by virtue of what will happen to him or her in adulthood. An unvaccinated child becomes a liability, so also one that has developed disabilities due to lack of basic care in early childhood. This person in adulthood may not be able to perform to their full capacity, and this, in turn, affects society.

Ron O'Grady, author of the famous book, *The Child and the Tourist*, stated very graphically that, "The way society treats its most vulnerable members is a measure of that society."[2] This essentially boils down to how society treats its children. As I write this, the news is full of cases of gross abuse of children in different parts of the world. While such cases are rampant in Asia where I lived and worked, the problem is just as serious elsewhere in the so-called

....

1   Global Forum for Child Survival, Atlanta, GA, Carter Center, 1996.
2   Ron O'Grady. *The Child and the Tourist: The Story Behind the Escalation of Child Prostitution in Asia* (Auckland, New Zealand: ECPAT, 1992).

developed world! Perhaps everywhere, there needs to be a serious examination of the status of children and the way they are cared for and considered during the development process.

Abuse is perhaps not the only problem that children have to cope with as they grow up. In less-developed countries, they often struggle to cope with less-than-conducive physical environments while growing up. In more-developed countries, they must often cope with less-than-conducive emotional environments, such as their parent's inability to cope in their relationships with each other. A fresh effort is therefore needed across the globe to bring the child back into the center of our care and concern. This is a first step.

Additional efforts also need to move beyond being "child-centered" to "child-focused." This is the next step, and it involves moving beyond the child's present needs for care and nurture to the child's future, long-term sustainability needs. It involves looking at all aspects of the development program to see how they will bring out the full potential of the child as an adult. One essential element of this is to also consider what the child's perspective of his or her future is, rather than just the adult's perspective on it. Early childhood development specialists tell us that most child development happens in the very first years of childhood. This, therefore, indicates that the child has the ability to contribute some useful and important insights into his or her development!

How is one to go about this, then? Obviously, if the child has the ability to give us useful insights, we have to find ways and means to enable the child to share those perspectives with us.

The United Nations Children's Fund (UNICEF) states,

> *Child participation involves encouraging and enabling children to make their views known on the issues that affect them. Put into practice, participation is adults listening to children—to their entire multiple and varied ways of communicating. It ensures their freedom to express themselves and takes their views into account when coming to decisions that affect them. Engaging children in dialogue and exchange allows them to learn constructive ways of influencing the world around them.*

> *Child participation must be authentic and meaningful. It must start with children and young people themselves, on their own terms, within their*

own realities and in pursuit of their own visions, dreams, hopes and concerns. Most of all, authentic and meaningful child participation requires a radical shift in adult thinking and behavior—from an exclusionary to an inclusionary approach to children and their capabilities.

The drive to participate is innate in every human being. Promoting meaningful and quality participation of children and adolescents is essential to ensuring their growth and development. Children have proved that when they are involved, they can make a difference in the world around them. They have ideas, experiences and insights that enrich adult understanding and make a positive contribution to adult actions."[3]

I have written before on child participation in *Participatory Poverty Alleviation and Development.*[4] I discussed the topic only briefly, however, because the book covered a wide range of issues related to participatory poverty alleviation and development. Recently, in the Yunnan province of the People's Republic of China, where I was facilitating a workshop, I observed some of the struggles of the staff in carrying out Participatory Learning and Action (PLA) activities with children. Nevertheless, with a little help and support, they soon got underway and were able to collect a lot of information from the group of children. The quality of participation and the response of the adults in the community when we shared the results with them was all the inspiration I needed to start writing this book!

The information in this book is relevant for all types of children and communities, including children facing specific challenges like disabilities and homelessness. I have also tried to introduce the reader with prevailing views to the subject of child participation, along with a rationale for it and some important principles and strategies involved. I have tried deliberately not to run straight into the various techniques involved, but instead to provide some basic insights into understanding certain realities like the Household Food Security Status (HHFSS) of the family, the contextual predeterminants, and prevailing societal attitudes and circumstances, all of which have an impact on the degree to which children can participate.

....

3   UNICEF, *State of the World's Children 2003: Child Participation* (Geneva: UNICEF, 2002).
4   Khon Kaen, Thailand: World Vision International—China, 2003. Also available as a CD-ROM from www.map.org.

One of the biggest deterrents to child participation is the prevailing attitude of the adult community to the value of their involvement in the affairs of the community and the development process. Sometimes it is necessary to show

the community that their perceptions are different from the perceptions of the children, and that the thoughts of children are valid and meaningful. That often helps move the concept of child participation from being a "joke" to something that is serious. Attitude change is crucial to the process, just as with any other participatory process. That attitude change has to start with us as agents of change and overflow to the community until we are all ready to involve children. We must strive to listen and learn from them, to understand their perspectives, and to make the kinds of changes that can influence their lives.

As I worked on the outline for this book, I sent it to several friends around the world who are working in development programs especially focused on children. The ensuing dialogue with friends particularly struggling with ways to increase child participation resulted in adding several sections to the book. I have tried to make it as comprehensive as possible to be of use for those working closely with children, whether they are in development programs or in academic institutions.

THE SCOPE OF THIS BOOK

I have deliberately attempted to keep the scope of this book quite broad. The topics covered are very comprehensive, and span a wide range of issues related to children. My hope in doing this is to provide a resource to organizations that work with children not only in rural areas, but also in urban communities. Some parts of the book are also relevant to schools. I hope that some of the more modern schools that work on an outcomes-based education system will use parts of the book as a guide to understand the world of children from their perspective. The basic principles involved in carrying out these exploratory exercises is the same, hence we can adapt them for use in different contexts.

Children have their own world, and have concerns and aspirations just like adults. The contexts in which they live influence them considerably, either limiting and retarding their progress or enhancing it. For example, the Household Food Security Status of a child's home has a strong impact on the way that child thinks and perceives reality. It also seriously affects their vulnerability. Similarly, their society's attitude toward education (such as its usefulness and appropriateness, especially for girl children) affects dropout rates. In some communities, children may need to share in their parents' workload. There may be creative ways of building this into the curriculum so work experience comes in as part of the learning input.

In the following pages, we will learn about how to understand the context of each child. Development practitioners, advocates, and children can use this information to bring about necessary changes in the community. The book also describes a wide range of participatory tools for working with children. Each tool has examples and an analysis to help you understand how to use the information strategically and effectively.

CHILD PARTICIPATION AND COMMUNITY DEVELOPMENT

More and more organizations are realizing that to serve children better, they need to learn more about how children perceive the world around them.

In the past, when organizations said they worked with children, what they essentially meant was that they were "child-centered." This meant they had a set of minimum standards and tried to make sure that every child in their care had or received each standard. Health experts or even child specialists externally determined these minimum standards (or "safety nets," as referred to by others). Ensuring a minimum package was available also had other complications, namely that it often made parents and guardians of children become dependent on an external agency for meeting the needs of their children. While the minimum standards package was a good yardstick to go by, it did not take other aspects into account.

This was overcome when organizations deliberately determined to become more innovative with their programs to make them child-focused, i.e., they started considering all development activities from the perspective of long-term impact on the life of children in the community.

For example, when they considered making a road, they also determined the long-term impact on children—whether it would open avenues for them for going to school or create access to healthcare and better opportunities. As much as possible, they considered aspects related to unintended impacts at the design phase and during program monitoring and evaluation. If the community had no schools, and though there was no immediate production benefits from constructing it, they considered it from a child-focused perspective as a priority, because it would have long-term benefits for children.

However, the community conducted all of these assessments entirely without consulting the children. The assumption here was that *children do not know what is best for them; hence, they cannot give useful inputs into the process.* This is not true. As those who make use of various development services and provisions, children can provide relevant insights on what is best for them.

A few years ago, I was invited by the Central Building Research Institute (CBRI) to be part of an evaluation team assessing the suitability of various innovative models of school buildings in Andhra Pradesh.

The government had undertaken a very creative initiative. They had contacted some of the top designers in the country as well as the institutes and organizations involved with low-cost housing technology and asked them to design school buildings in rural areas. After around twenty-five of these buildings were ready, the government asked the CBRI to make an evaluation of each model and identify a few of them that would be ideal for replication around the state.

One of the aspects of this evaluation was to find out the community's perspective. CBRI asked me to train the sociologists in the team in using participatory tools for making the assessments. While doing this, I added on a component for getting the perspective of children regarding the design of the school buildings. Our findings were surprising. The children had plenty to say about the designs, including pointing out inadequacies. These were especially in the area of ventilation, natural light illumination, damp flooring, and leaking roofs.

At the end of the exercise, we presented our findings to the group. All of us were surprised at how strongly the children felt about the issues. We asked them if they would like to have a dialogue with the technical team of architects and civil engineers and they agreed. Later, when we arranged this, it was interesting to watch the looks on the faces of the engineers as they sat across the room from a group of primary school children, listening to their assessments about the new school building compared to the old classrooms they had used earlier. When the children got to the stage where they were pointing out changes that could be made, the dialogue shifted. The sociologists and I no longer served as the go betweens, but instead, the children and engineers dialogued directly. The two groups were soon moving around the building, pointing and discussing animatedly—like equals!

The climax of the whole meeting was when an engineer replied to the children's recommendations, "How are we supposed to make this modification?" The reply was instant: "We are only telling you what we want . . . You are the expert; you should know how to do it!"

Children have views and definite perspectives on things that affect them. We need to provide ways for their voices to be heard. Just sitting them down in a meeting with adults is not enough. How can we encourage all children— even the most marginalized—to share, letting them know that their opinion is important and valued? How can we help them to feel comfortable sharing their opinions in a variety of settings?

This is the purpose of this book. After discussing some of the rationale for children's participation and the need to understand some basic factors, the rest of this book concentrates on various aspects of mobilizing the participation of children.

Several Participatory Learning and Action (PLA) tools are described here. Some of these have been modified and adapted for use with children, while others are brand-new. In addition to the PLA techniques mentioned here, there are some additional pieces related to the importance of play for children. Children must have time to play and enjoy themselves. I have mentioned how a profile of the games children play can be created. They have very vivid imaginations and can be very creative in finding ways to play even with limited resources. The lack of rules for a game is not a limitation for them, as they can easily create new rules.

Drama is another important way to communicate and begin discussions. We have used drama especially with street children, giving them the basic plot and asking them to dramatize it. During the last scene, the characters are told to sit back at their locations and the outcome is discussed, including looking at alternate scenarios. I have discussed this at length in a later section. Years ago, on a visit to see The Carter Center in Atlanta, I saw the use of hand puppets in the head start program and how the agency used them to generate the topic of study for the day, with the active involvement of the children.

How do children perceive the way they are treated at home and in school? Discrimination, or even a perception that they are being discriminated against, can leave children with scars for life. I have also discussed ways and means to find this out, including the differences in the way boy children and girl children perceive themselves as being treated.

Involving children in the monitoring and evaluation process is also important, because it legitimizes their role in the process. How to do this creatively is another aspect the book covers.

As I wrote this, back in Cambodia, almost daily, the local newspapers were reporting cases of child abuse. CNN aired a special feature entitled "Easy Prey," which was a shocking documentary about children in trafficking and sexual exploitation. The issue of child abuse is a stark reality of our times. How often does it happen in the villages where we work? To what extent are children affected? How much of it is condoned or swept under the carpet for the sake of family or village honor? These are questions not only for Asia, but also for all over the world where people work.

Finally, for the first time ever, the use of a Holistic Worldview Analysis (HWVA) of the children's world is also discussed at length. This is a consolidated picture of the world of children, drawn from the child's perspective and including their place and role. This exercise provides a baseline of how things stand, and practitioners can use it to monitor progress over time. Since this is a profile of what the children initially perceived as their world, it is also good to keep some blank segments to add in future as they become conscious of more aspects of their world.

Also, the placement of the seeds in the second concentric circle (controlled by parents/adults) may often be considerable, showing us that they see their world controlled by adults. At times of monitoring, negotiations between the children and parents can be facilitated to allow greater control to children.

The HWVA of the children can then also be used to analyze their survival strategy to consider its capacities and vulnerabilities. As in the case with the HWVA of a community, areas of greatest vulnerability can be prioritized. This can help design a Children's Participation Plan, with a listing of actions to be taken and names of those responsible with their respective tasks. This action plan can be prepared in a simple way to be understood by children. copies can be given to each member of the community, including the children.

What is being suggested here is not mere lip service or even attendance of children, but full-fledged involvement and the ability to make a positive contribution to impact and improve their world. What the book suggests and also shows ways of doing practically is full engagement!

I have tried to make everything mentioned in this book as practical and down-to-earth as possible so those who are keen to learn and use the techniques can do so. Let me encourage you about something else. You do not have to have a university degree to understand how to use Participatory Learning and Action with children. Having a concern and interest is a beginning, but attitude change is mandatory for success!

RATIONALE FOR INVOLVING CHILDREN IN DEVELOPMENT

Is there a valid rationale for involving children in development? Is this just the fancy (and perhaps unrealistic) dream of some idealist? Or is it merely the current "fashion" doing its rounds in development circles?

Yes, I do believe with all my heart that there is a valid rationale for involving children in the process of identifying their concerns for their own development and also for involving them in the entire process. This is definitely not just idealistic nor is it something that is being suggested because it is the latest watchword among leading organizations involved in child-focused development. Children are an important part of society, and how they are treated and valued is an important indicator of their community. When a community invests its resources in its children, it is essentially investing in its own future and furthering its own survival strategy. Investing in children promotes long-term sustainability.

In addition, children have the right to participate. Articles 9, 12, and 23 of the United Nations *Convention on the Rights of the Child* declare that children, including kids with disabilities, have the right to participate fully in their communities and in decisions that involve them.[5] The Convention also strongly emphasizes that "the best interests of the child shall be a primary

....

5   Geneva: United Nations, 1989, http://www2.ohchr.org/english/law/crc.htm.

consideration" for all things that affect them.[6] How better to empower children and act in their best interests than to ask for their input? When an investing  agent wants to invest his or her client's finances, the ultimate stakeholder—the client—must be consulted. Why then does it seem unreasonable to find out from children what their perspectives and concerns are? Perhaps the whole idea sounds ridiculous to some people because they wonder what useful contribution children can make. This assumption is probably because they feel that children are too immature to know what they want, and that adults should therefore do their thinking for them!

During some PLA exercises conducted recently in south China, this became immensely clear. First, PLA exercises were conducted with a group of parents, with the goal of finding out what the parents saw as challenges for the children in their community. The parents identified two primary challenges:

1. the inability of the parents to send the children to school or university; and
2. the poor nutritional status of the children.

Other challenges included the inability to speak Mandarin when they first got to school (since the community primarily used the indigenous language of their minority group), insufficient clothes, and time wasted watching television.

When this was shared with the larger group, they also agreed that these were the problems faced by children. When the same exercise was conducted with children to find out what they were "unhappy" about,[7] they identified four primary challenges:

1. the poor results they got in school;
2. the fact that their parents did not buy them the things they wanted;
3. the punishments and scolding they received from their parents; and
4. the inability to sleep properly at night.

....

6   United Nations, *Convention on the Rights of the Child*, "Article 3."
7   We used the term "unhappy" because asking them "what problems they faced" did not make sense to them.

It turned out that the perspectives of the children were considerably different from their parents' perspectives. We then used the exercise to explore further what children liked to do. The response was immediate, graphic, clear, and emphatic. They loved going to school and doing housework to help their parents with domestic chores. In addition, they loved playing and planting flowers. Watching the reactions of the community to this information was very interesting. They kept discussing among themselves and looking with wonder at their children!

From a Christian perspective, the realization that all children have dignity and are created in the image of God helps us to see that children's input is valuable. The Bible's concepts of community, church, and mission further help us to see that God not only uses children in his wonderful plan but that he also wants all of his children—male, female, young, and old—to participate in his work in the world.[8] Think about Joseph, Miriam, Samuel, David, Naaman's slave girl, Esther, Mary, and even Jesus himself. God used each of these individuals while they were still children to change entire nations! Surely, we should value children's participation and encourage them to be involved in the development process as well.

Children understand their world very well. They know how to share this information if the process is appropriately facilitated, and their participation is both a right and a biblical emphasis. Mobilizing children's participation is not very difficult, but the results can be extraordinary because the children will immediately realize that their concerns are being addressed.

....

8   For more on these concepts, see Douglas McConnell, Jennifer Orona, and Paul Stockley, eds., *Understanding God's Heart for Children: Toward a Biblical Framework* (Colorado Springs: Authentic, 2007), especially chapters 1, 6, and 7.

PREPARATION

* * *

Lesson 1:
KEY PRINCIPLES

R EADING UP TO this point must have given you a clear idea that involving children in the development process is not mere "child's play!" Using participatory tools with children for involving them closely in the development process requires a well-planned strategy. Again, these are not intended to be "one-size-fits-all" models. At best, these concepts can serve as guiding principles and strategies for use. Please feel free to modify and adapt them to your own context.

KEY PRINCIPLES OF CHILD PARTICIPATION

Two resources demonstrate the key principles that should be used as you work to mobilize and empower children to participate in various activities. Tearfund's Wheel of Participation encourages you first to give children respect, and then to give support, responsibility, and opportunity.[9]

Roger Hart's "Ladder of Young People's Participation" gives further descriptions of what types of actions and attitudes truly empower children's participation and what types are just manipulations, tokenism, or decoration instead of true participation.[10]

As you read the following lessons on preparation and try out the exercises in this book, keep these principles in mind. You may want to refer back to this section as you and your team plan activities and design exercises to learn with children. Think about how you can respectfully support children and give them opportunities to share their thoughts, initiate action, and make joint decisions with adults.

....

9   Paul Stephenson with Steve Gourley and Glenn Miles, *Child Participation* (Teddington, UK: Tearfund, 2004), 14, http://tilz.tearfund.org/Publications/ROOTS/Child+participation.htm.
10   Roger Hart, *Children's Participation: From Tokenism to Citizenship* (Florence: UNICEF Innocenti Research Centre, 1992). See also http://www.freechild.org/ladder.htm.

KEY PRINCIPLES FOR DEVELOPING A PILOT PROGRAM

Let us now turn our attention to several of the important principles involved. The following are five key principles for success in developing a pilot program.

1.
First, convince yourself that children's participation is a good idea.

First of all, it is important that *you* are convinced that involving children in the development process is important and a good idea. Do as much reading as possible on the subject of child participation.[11] Also, talk to experienced educators who are open to new concepts. If there are organizations that have already started work like this in your area, visit them, observe their work, and learn from their experiences, especially about their struggles while getting started. After you are convinced and have studied enough about the techniques, identify a project location where you can launch your pilot program.

2.
Mobilize support within the community for the venture.

At the pilot program site, arrange for a meeting with the community elders and leaders, and talk with them briefly about the concept. You can use some of the examples from this book to talk to them about some of the perspectives of children and how they have impacted and modified the intervention. Prepare well for carrying out one or two simple exercises to demonstrate the effectiveness of the techniques. List the advantages of the program and mobilize their support for it, including a commitment from them that they will follow through on the findings and support the actions that might be needed. During this exercise, stories and case studies from other projects will come in very handy. There are plenty of examples quoted in this book that can be used for

....

11   An internet search on "child participation" will help access a great number of articles on the subject. Also, please see www.celebratingchildrentraining.info; www.knowingchildren.org; and http://tilz.tearfund.org/Publications/ROOTS/Child+participation.htm.

this purpose. Once this has been done, set dates and begin your program! Soon, you will have your own pictures, stories, and successes to quote.

3.
Get enough experience to demonstrate and share in new areas.

After completing the exercises in one community, your confidence will be built up. Succeeding communities will then be much easier to work in. You will have several examples to draw from, and very soon you will have the confidence to meet members of a new community, demonstrate the techniques with the children, and analyze the information for the community.

KEY PRINCIPLES

1. Get yourself convinced that children's participation is a good idea.
2. Mobilize support within the community for the venture.
3. Get enough experience to demonstrate and share in new areas.
4. Generate examples of success to share.
5. Be prepared to become a hub of sharing and learning.

4.
Generate examples of success to share.

When several locations have started using the techniques, these pilot projects can become centers of learning and demonstration of the concept. The experiences from these places can be documented and recorded for sharing with others. When coupled with testimonials about experiences from people who were involved in the process, photographs showing the process are very good ways of convincing the audience. Never hesitate to be candid about some of your own doubts and struggles when starting. Case studies and specific learning that came about through understanding the perspective of children can also be a strong support while introducing the approach in new places.

When you get started, take plenty of pictures. With today's modern technology of digital photography, this should be very easy. Sequential photographs taken as an exercise is in progress are an excellent tool to show people how the exercise is conducted and how attitudes can change. Finally, nothing breeds success like success itself! Arrange field visits to places where the program is operating, and facilitate interaction with the community so that they can talk with the "outsiders" and share their experiences.

CHILD PROTECTION WHILE TAKING PICTURES

It is very important to be aware of child protection issues when taking pictures. Here are a few tips:

1. Always ask the children for permission to take and use photos.
2. If possible, ask parents or guardians for permission as well.
3. Do not use photos of children if this could lead to harm for them (e.g., if you are working with children who are survivors of sexual exploitation).
4. Do not use photos of sad or dirty faces just to ask people for money.

5.
Prepare to become a hub of sharing and learning.

The concept is still very new, so you have every chance of becoming a pioneer in your area. Some people may ask if they can come to visit your project so that they can learn from you. I have noticed of late that several organizations are reluctant to have people come and visit their projects and consider such visits an intrusion on their time. Always remember that sharing your experiences can also result in growth for you! When you give to others, you also receive back from them, and this in turn becomes a means for your growth. This has always been a hallmark of participatory techniques. When PLA techniques began in the mid-1980s, many people were quick to share their learning with others. It is this that helped make it a global movement. Today, almost every donor[12] insists that the technique should be actively used in their programs. In future years, I believe that trends in development will be such as to have a lot to do with creating infrastructure in the rural areas, transitioning from microenterprise to small business development, and the incorporation of innovative approaches and interventions into current educational programs. These interventions will take current educational programs far beyond the mere creation of educational facilities to innovative interventions for curriculum development and more!

MINIMUM STANDARDS FOR CHILD PARTICIPATION

In addition, you will need to keep in mind a set of minimum standards for child participation. The following list has been developed by Save the Children for people who work directly with children. These standards seek to ensure that children are adequately protected, that the staff is well prepared, that all children are treated with equality, and that activities are followed up and evaluated properly.[13]

Standard 1: An ethical approach: transparency and honesty
Adult organizations and workers are committed to ethical participatory practice and to the primacy of children's best interests.

This means that, as mentioned previously, the best interests of the children need to be a primary concern. Also, adults need to be *ethical* (morally upright) in their behavior.

....

12   Donors include the World Bank, the Asian Development Bank (ADB), United States Agency for International Development (USAID), the Australian Agency for International Development (AusAID), the United Kingdom's Department for International Development (DFID), and various United Nations agencies.
13   These minimum standards are taken from Save the Children, *Practice Standards in Child Participation* (London: Save the Children, n.d.), 4–11, http://www.savethechildren.net/alliance/about_us/accountability/practicestandardscp.doc.

Standard 2: Children's participation is relevant and voluntary

Children participate in work on issues that directly affect them and have the choice as to whether to participate or not.

Make sure that children are invited to participate in the things that affect and interest them, and never coerce or manipulate children to make them participate.

Standard 3: A child friendly, enabling environment

Children experience a safe, welcoming and encouraging environment for their participation.

This is more than just saying hello to each child, it includes training your team and the community in how to keep information confidential, treat children with respect, and truly listen to what children have to say.

Standard 4: Equality of opportunity

Child participation work should challenge and not reinforce existing patterns of discrimination and exclusion.

Can children with disabilities participate in your activities? Are girls and boys treated fairly? The exercises and activities that your team facilitates should be a role model to the community of giving all children equal opportunities.

Standard 5: Staff members are effective and confident

Adult staff and managers involved in work on children's participation are trained and supported to do their jobs to a high standard.

It is far better to spend extra time training and preparing with your team than to jump headfirst into an activity and do it poorly. Also, make sure that your team has the resources and time that they need to do their best.

Standard 6: Participation promotes the safety and protection of children

Child protection policy and procedures form an essential part of participatory work with children.

You will need to review your organization's child protection policy with your team before doing any activities with children. Think through specific ways that your team will need to be aware of child protection issues.[14]

Standard 7: Follow-up and evaluation

Respect for children's involvement is indicated by commitment to provide feedback and/or follow-up and to evaluate the quality and impact of children's participation.

Finally, you will need to keep track of the information that you collect, share it with the children and the community, and invite children to be involved in follow-up, monitoring, and evaluation.

....
14   For more on child protection policies, see http://www.keepingchildrensafe.org.uk/.

* * *

Lesson 2:
ESSENTIAL STRATEGIES

THE FOLLOWING ARE some recommended strategies:

1.
Recognize and help others to recognize the value of
involving children.

This element is so important that it bears repeating. Perhaps the best way to accomplish this is through finding persons within organizations who can serve as champions for promoting this cause in the initial stages. When you share the concept or invite someone to your organization to talk about the active participation of children in the development process, be on the lookout for those who get excited about the idea and who have a good focus on children's well-being. From among these people, you will probably find the person with the potential to be a champion.

Work to equip this person by providing them with opportunities for further exposure on the subject. If you serve in a leadership position, free the person up for a period of time to be able to focus on the task of marketing the idea and convincing people that it is not a passing fad! The champion should strive to identify people who are open to new ideas, and then spend time sharing with them. Ensure that everyone knows that the idea has *management support*, because this will help both the champion and others to recognize how important this new idea is for the entire organization. The champion should also identify a project manager who is willing to take on additional work and willing to launch the pilot project in his or her area. The following steps will apply directly to the champion.

Essential Strategies for the Champion for Children's Participation

1. Recognize and help others to recognize the value of involving children.
   - Learn as much as you can about involving children in the development process.
   - Identify and share with project leaders and others who are open to new ideas.
   - Look for a location to launch a pilot project.

2. Get ready to launch a pilot project.
   - Identify a critical mass of people.
   - Make sure that you have management support before you begin.
   - Team up with other organizations.
   - Launch the pilot project.

3. Reach out to more areas.
   - Develop new initiatives in new locations.
   - Hold regular team meetings.
   - Work to become part of a network.

4. Rally support from stakeholders and decision makers.
   - Inform the media.
   - Share your experiences with stakeholders and decision makers.
   - Be prepared to combine new methods with traditional methods until policy change takes place.

5. Regulate and ratify the approach.
   - After launching out in fifteen to twenty projects, develop a set of agreed-upon guidelines and strategies.
   - Set aside specific times for sharing.
   - Look for patterns of good practices.
   - Work to regulate and ratify these into flexible guidelines.

6. Replicate the practices and share information with others.
   - Record your experiences.
   - Share the information with others in your organization, region, and network.
   - Keep developing new methods!

2.
Get ready to launch a pilot project.

As soon as a critical mass of people[15] in the organization is identified and you have the support and blessing of the management to move forward, then it is time to launch the pilot project! I strongly recommend that the launch must have management support, because the findings of the study may require changes and modifications in the way you work in the field. Without management support, this flexibility will not be there, and may result in frustration for all involved. Therefore, if you do not have management support, continue to wait until you have it. In the meantime, you can gather more information to convince the management if that is the challenge. It may not always be possible for you to launch a pilot project as a single organization, and even if it were possible, it would still be wise to team up with other organizations. Again, if you cannot take the lead in this due to lack of support, you can support a different organization that is taking the lead. Continue to prepare yourself and your team by reading, visiting, and sharing during times of waiting.

Next, launch the pilot project! Use the strategies, concepts, and ideas throughout this book to involve children in the development of a new program, or in reworking a program that is already in progress. You could also facilitate children's participation in evaluating a current project. Make sure to keep good records, including notes on successes and challenges, photos (if possible), and stories that can serve as examples for future projects.

3.
Reach out to more areas.

When you have successfully launched your program, reach out to more areas and more organizations to develop new initiatives. These will provide you with a variety of experiences that will help you to better understand the issues involved, and will also give you several examples at different locations. Provide regular opportunities for team meetings so that *lateral learning* (learning from

....

15   A critical mass is a good enough number of people to have influence. In many cases, this needs to be at least 10 percent of the staff. In others, especially if there are strong opinion leaders on your side, a critical mass can be achieved with fewer people.

peers) can take place. This way, staff can learn from members of their own organization, along with members of other organizations.

Eventually, your team can work to become part of a network that spans the country or the region.[16] Be proactive in doing this. It is quite possible that you may have to take the lead in creating the network. The interest within this network will also vary over time. Initially, many may be interested in the concept of launching out. At later stages, the discussions will heat up as issues like curriculum development emerge, and new resources and information for educators and other experts will need to be added.[17]

4.
Rally support from stakeholders and decision makers.

Invite journalists to observe the innovations and publish several articles in the newspaper to encourage the interest of the local community and key leaders. Then, using examples and some basic documentation of what has happened, share your experiences with stakeholders and decision makers. You can even invite them to visit a field site to gain some personal experience. This is an ideal way to develop relationships and help them to see the value of child participation. Of course, opportunities for policy changes will come only after the program has been adopted on a very wide scale. Until policy changes take place, the approach will be to have a combination of the traditional and the new methods.

5.
Regulate and ratify the approach.

Even before policy changes are brought into effect, it is helpful to create a set of agreed-upon guidelines and strategies for your team. This should only be done after the program has been launched for some time, and the well-being of children should be a central consideration in this process. Experiences will vary from organization to organization and from location to location, so exact

....

16   For a list of networks in your region, please visit www.viva.org.
17   I believe that this will also become a new trend in the future as more NGOs graduate from merely being involved in service provision (making school buildings or teaching staff) to getting involved with designing curricula.

timeframes will vary as well. My recommendation is that you do not consider doing this until you have launched out in at least fifteen to twenty locations.

A good idea is to set aside specific times for sharing. During team meetings, experience-sharing sessions, and field visits, definite patterns will emerge, and you will begin to see which practices are most successful in your context. Once the team has identified effective patterns and practices, work to regulate and ratify them. This regulation and ratification should only be in the form of guidelines so that there is enough flexibility for adaptation to locally varying contexts.

EXPERIENCE-SHARING WORKSHOP

A three-day workshop can help the team to share experiences, consolidate learning, and develop a set of agreed-upon guidelines, strategies, and approaches.

To help your team regulate and ratify their approach, you can put together a three-day experience-sharing workshop. Here are a few strategies to consider as you plan your workshop:

- *Enlist the help of an experienced facilitator to draw out the learning.* This is an invaluable asset since the team members come from a variety of backgrounds, experiences, and organizations. The facilitator can help to make sure that each voice is heard, that the group remains focused, and that the guidelines accurately reflect the experiences of the team.

- *Include time for building relationships.* As you develop the schedule for the workshop, intentionally make time in the schedule for team members to get to know one another on a deeper level.

- On the final day of the workshop, *invite an experienced and innovative educator to help synthesize the learning.* Ideally, this will be a person with experience in nonformal education, since they will be familiar with the types of situations that many of the children live in. This person can help the group to put their thoughts on paper, consolidate the information, and write down the guidelines, strategies, and approaches that will form the foundation for future policies.

6.
Replicate the practices and share information with others.

As mentioned earlier, this is a new field and there is a lot of need for information and expertise. When experience becomes available, it should be shared with others. I hope you will be a pioneer and lead the movement in your areas so that special attention can be given to facilitating marginalized and poor children to bring out the best in them.

* * *

Lesson 3:
UNDERSTANDING REALITIES: HOUSEHOLD FOOD SECURITY STATUS

IN CONSIDERING WHAT is best for the children, we have to consider the realities in which they live. For some families, even the most modest possessions and services remain out of reach. For example, we might ensure that a school building intended for a particular community is constructed in the poorest part of town so that the children of the poorest families can go to school easily. The circumstances of the poorest families, however, may determine that their children must work to supplement the family income, or that the children must take care of household chores, younger siblings, and animals while their parents go to work. Thus, the school, which may be constructed just a few feet from their homes, may be out of reach. In some cases, the same thing can happen with the creation of healthcare facilities or even agriculture input support[18] if the family has had to mortgage their land to a moneylender to pay bills and can no longer farm their own land for income.

Experience in the field has taught us that the Household Food Security Status (HHFSS) plays an important role in determining the extent to which a household can benefit from services and facilities created for them.[19] For this reason, I recommend performing a basic HHFSS assessment for the community before proceeding with any of the other exercises in this book.

....

18   E.g., fertilizers, seeds, insecticides, and so on.
19   This subject is discussed at length in another book which I authored, *Participatory Poverty Alleviation and Development*. I will explain the concepts here in brief.

CARRYING OUT A HOUSEHOLD FOOD SECURITY STATUS ASSESSMENT IN A COMMUNITY

Invite a group from the community—both adults and children—to gather together with you. Choose community members who are aware of the community and its situation. First, you will need to spend some time building rapport and explaining the purpose of the exercise (to understand the Household Food Security Status of the community). You will also want to explain the Ten-Seed Technique and how it is used for this exercise.[20]

The Ten-Seed Technique

In the Ten-Seed Technique, the group is shown ten seeds and asked to consider them to represent all the households in the community. Next, they are asked to divide the seeds into two groups, one representing those households in the community that are easily able to meet their needs for the whole year, and the other representing the households in the community that have a struggle meeting their needs. The seeds are to be divided to show the representative portions of the community households that fall into the two categories.

USING THE TEN-SEED TECHNIQUE

Most of the time, the idea becomes clearer and the group catches on during the first few questions. Initially, there is often great reluctance to move the seeds, but once the first move is made almost everyone is ready to get involved! Allow time for these modifications. You will learn to recognize when the group feels it agrees on the proportions, as they will sound happy and relaxed about their decisions.

Let us assume that the seeds are placed in the following proportion (as seen in the following diagram): Two seeds represent those who are able to

....

20   For more information on the Ten-Seed Technique, see Ravi Jayakaran, "TST—Ten-Seed Technique," http://www.fao.org/Participation/ft_show.jsp?ID=1981 and Ravi Jayakaran, "The Ten-Seed Technique: Learning How the Community Sees Itself," *Child Survival Connections* (Spring 2002), http://www.childsurvival.com/connections/Connections_Spring%202002.pdf.

meet their needs for the whole year, while eight seeds represent the households that have difficulty meeting their needs for the whole year.

Households that are able to meet their 'needs' for the whole year.	● ●
Households that have struggles to meet their 'needs' for the whole year.	● ● ● ● ● ● ● ●

The next step will be to encourage the group to further divide the second set of seeds. From my observations in several countries, the seeds usually get divided into two or three further subgroups, and very rarely, into four subgroups. Allow time for discussion, rearrangements, and modifications. Again, agreement in the group will be followed by the group being happy and relaxed. It is essential to have consensus on this, so if there are disagreements, allow the group some more time to come to an agreement. Let us assume that the seeds are divided as follows:

Households that are able to meet their 'needs' for the whole year.	A. ● ●
Households that have struggles to meet their 'needs' for the whole year.	B. ● ● ●
	C. ● ● ●
	D. ● ●

In the diagram above, the second set of seeds (representing the households in the community that have struggles making ends meet), are divided into three subgroups. The group is asked to explain their reasoning, and they explain that it is according to the amount of time each year during which they have struggles. The first group of seeds (B) represents the households that are able to generally meet their needs, but struggle to do so for one to two months in the year. The second group of seeds (C) represents those households that can generally meet their needs, but struggle to do so for three to five months in the year. Finally, the last group (D) represents those households in the community that have struggles *throughout the year* to meet their needs. The group is then asked to identify the local name by which each of the categories A, B, C, and D are known in the community. In most cases, each category will have specific names and profiles that extend even to the types of houses they live in.

Categorizing the Households

The following diagram illustrates the specific types of situations for this example, and how they can be classified accordingly:

Household Food Security Status		
Number of Seeds	Vulnerability Status	Description
● ●	Above the Prosperity line	Those who have no struggles to meet their needs
● ● ●	(just above) Poverty line	Those who generally are able to meet their needs, but struggle for 1 to 2 months in a year
● ● ●	(just below) Poverty line	Those who generally are able to meet their needs, but struggle for 3 to 5 months in a year
● ●	Below the Charity line	Those who struggle throughout the year to meet their needs

HHFSS assessments SE Asia/RJ/QPI

The first group constitutes what can be referred to as the one that is *above the prosperity line*. This group continues to prosper and benefit whatever happens in the community, because their surplus enables them to invest in further increasing their income and creating assets. This group has spare resources to invest in their children because their thinking has become futuristic. They will therefore be the first to make use of all programs for the benefit of children. The second group—referred to as the one just above the poverty line—is one that is upwardly mobile and strives to continuously emulate the first group. They, too, will be able to access most programs for the benefit of their children.

The third group is where a greater number of challenges begin. The deficit they experience in meeting needs cannot be overcome with resilience, hence they end up in debt every year, depending on future production to cover current needs. This *below the poverty line* group finds it very hard to regularly access the programs that will benefit their children. Even when they are able to access the programs, their access is erratic—regularly during the good months, and irregularly during the difficult months. This inconsistency begins to affect the children and retards their progress for reasons beyond their own

efforts. The final group is referred to as the one *below the charity line*. By the time a household reaches this state, it has probably lost all of its productive resources or mortgaged them to the extent that they are no longer available to them for use. This situation results in an increasing demand for family members to become breadwinners, and children from this group are very likely to be drawn into the workforce, if they are not working already. Instead of being *receivers*, they have to become *providers*; and programs for them, no matter how excellent, remain out of reach. The following diagram makes the reason for this very clear:

Household Food Security Status			
Number of Seeds	Vulnerability Status	Balance Sheet	
		Income	Expenditure
● ●	Above the Prosperity line	● ● ● ● ●	● ● ● ●
● ● ●	(just above) Poverty line	● ● ● ● ●	● ● ● ● ●
● ● ●	(just below) Poverty line	● ● ● ●	● ● ● ● ●
● ●	Below the Charity line	● ● ●	● ● ● ● ● ● ●

HHFSS assessments SE Asia/RJ/QPI

The last columns here represent the balance sheet, as it were, showing the ratio between income and expenditure for each of the household categories. The surplus and shortage for each group are very clearly visible here. Surplus results in a willingness to invest in children, while shortage results in withdrawal from programs. When household expenditure exceeds income, things like education, care, and nurture of children suffer. Costs have to be cut in order to manage, so it is the urgent that takes precedence over the important—the present need instead of investing in the future. In the end, it is the children that are the greatest victims, getting locked in this poverty trap that isolates from the very programs that were designed for them!

The Violence of Excruciating Poverty

Gandhi Ji (M.K. Gandhi, who led India's freedom movement) said, "Poverty is the worst form of violence."[21] And indeed it is. At the level of those below the charity line, poverty is excruciating.

The next few diagrams are related to the way that these excruciating challenges —what I call the violence of excruciating poverty—strongly impact the context of households that fall into the lower levels of poverty. The first diagram relates to children who are "rag-pickers" (children who collect items to recycle from the trash, then sell the items for a small profit). While carrying out a "macro zoom PLA"[22] exercise related to what types of families these children came from, we learned that all of the families were migrants who had moved from rural areas to the urban slums. The finding here was that, although the children came from all categories of HHFSS, there was a higher concentration among those just above and just below the poverty line. Perhaps this occurred because rag-picking is a way to supplement the family's income without having to learn a difficult skill, and is easy to adopt (especially during times of transition).

Household Food Security Status Families from which rag-pickers come	
Vulnerability Status	Children staying at the garbage dumps
Above the Prosperity line	●
(just above) Poverty line	● ● ●
(just below) Poverty line	● ● ● ●
Below the Charity line	● ●

HHFSS assessments SE Asia/RJ/QPI

....

21   Mahatma Gandhi, "Mahatma Gandhi," http://www.cybernation.com/victory/quotations/ authors/quotes_gandhi_mahatma.html (accessed January 12, 2009).
22   A macro zoom PLA is a participatory learning and action exercise conducted at the broader macro level to understand an issue.

The disadvantage is that children end up spending much of their time on the streets. The street is a dangerous place with continuous exposure to drugs, crime, and the sex trade, and with their ability to learn quickly, children (even very young ones) will often adopt the ways of the street very quickly as well. It takes a long time indeed to get the "street out of them," even when their environment has been changed.

Nevertheless, there are several strengths that households below the poverty line experience. Some members of the group work to organize the household into some type of economic activity. Usually, they also have some degree of shelter, which leaves them less vulnerable than the next group.

Household Food Security Status Families from which street children come	
Food Security Status	Children on the streets
Above the Prosperity line	
(just above) Poverty line	
(just below) Poverty line	● ●
Below the Charity line	● ● ● ● ● ● ● ● ●

HHFSS assessments SE Asia/RJ/QPI

The next diagram is related to street children who live and survive on the streets. While in many ways they are similar to those shown in the first diagram, their condition is one of far greater vulnerability. The macro zoom PLA for this group showed that all of these children came from the third and fourth HHFSS categories, below the poverty line and below the charity line. The majority of the children came from households that were below the charity line. Studies have shown that as the household falls to the lower level in the HHFSS scale, there are no longer any social security scaffoldings to provide a safety net to the family.[23] Continuous poverty results in growing debt and an inability to meet even the basic needs. Often, the family breaks up quickly because of domestic discord resulting from financial difficulties. Ultimately, the children from these households end up on the streets, with no protection at all from its dangers.

For almost all of these children and their families, the challenges had already started before they migrated to the city slums. In the community, their poverty caused the reduction of their productive resources, and so they had to depend on alternative means of income, usually in the form of unskilled labor. As the family approached the point when it would have to migrate to the urban area, it also began to consider education as a luxury that it could ill afford. Thus, children from such households do not often get to go to school. If they are attending, they are withdrawn from school.

The final diagram in this series is one related to an analysis of the conditions that led to the commercial sexual exploitation of children:

Household Food Security Status

Families from which the children in CSW (Commercial Sex Worker) activity come

Food Security Status	Children involved with CSW activity	Reasons
Above the Prosperity line	●	children who were deceived or raped in their areas
(just above) Poverty line	● ●	children from reasonably secure families, but those that had a financial crisis like illness
(just below) Poverty line	● ● ● ●	families in debt or those with single income provider who is unable to cope with the needs . . . and actually decided to sell the child
Below the Charity line	● ● ●	destitute families

HHFSS assessments SE Asia/RJ/QPI

. . . .

23   Ravi Jayakaran, et al., "Studies of Food Security-Related Vulnerability," World Vision Asia Pacific Region, 2001.

Children who end up in the horrible trap of the commercial sex trade experience some of the worst possible situations. They are more abused, more traumatized, and more deprived of their rights than children in almost any other situation. This is a growing problem especially in South East Asia, as well as elsewhere in Asia, and in fact, all over the world.[24] Once again, children in families living below the poverty line and below the charity line are the most vulnerable.

The point that I am making here, therefore, is that when we consider undertaking a program that focuses on children, we must consider the realities of the context in which they live. The HHFSS is one such stark reality. We must understand and address all that it involves, working to add programs that are designed to overcome the challenges of each family's food security status. Some have said that poverty is a lack of freedom to grow and that we need to provide the necessary freedom to ensure that the children we seek to serve can access our services.

....

24   For more on this topic, please see www.asha.viva.org; www.ijm.org; www.love146.org; and www.chabdai.org.

* * *

Lesson 4:

UNDERSTANDING REALITIES: CIRCUMSTANCES

.

UNDERSTANDING THE REALITY of the circumstances of a community . . . this is so easy to say and yet so difficult to actually practice. As mentioned previously, the violence of excruciating poverty and Gandhi Ji's concept of poverty as the greatest form of violence point to the crippling influence of extreme poverty.

For Gandhi Ji, this was his motivating force to keep the founding fathers of post-freedom India focused on the needs of the poor and their poverty-ridden circumstances. A few years ago, in India, following a spate of suicides by desperate rural farmers, the Prime Minister, Dr. Manmohan Singh, visited villages where incidents had taken place to learn firsthand about what had happened. What he saw was a close-up view of their circumstances—the utter desperation of the circumstances that had compelled hundreds of hardworking villagers to end their lives. After spending time talking to the families of those who had died and other farmers in similar situations, Dr. Manmohan Singh observed that he had "never seen so much pain in the eyes of people before." Perhaps that is what we are called to do in understanding the marginalized— look into their eyes and see the realities of their circumstances.

Communities can find themselves in many difficult circumstances. These can have an overriding influence on the way they think and act, along with the way they make decisions related to their futures and the futures of their children. These circumstances are the results of a variety of factors. Let us now consider several of these factors.

Contextual Predeterminants

In an ideal world, every child would have the opportunity to study. All children would live in an environment where they would be encouraged to grow to their full potential. However, the world that we live in is far from perfect and the contextual realities in each child's environment may hold them back. Despite our best efforts, some children may not be able to come to school at the same time as all the others. *This may be because of contextual predeterminants.*

As seen previously, by the time a family's Household Food Security Status drops below the poverty line or below the charity line, their control over productive resources has dwindled. This means that the family now has to rely on what they have left—namely, *human resources*. Their source of income and livelihood has also gradually been transitioning from a combination of reduced production and service provision, to a stage where it is almost entirely service provision. The demand on labor thus increases, and every hand that is available must be put to work. Thus, the working child becomes a reality in such homes, and there may be no other way for the family to adopt in order to keep their family together.

These families will almost certainly require assistance to overcome their situation. While assistance may often have to be in the form of major interventions, development workers are increasingly finding that helping families who are below the charity line is a mammoth task that requires large amounts of capital and labor. The transition time involved is also long, and therefore, alternatives need to be developed, such as making nonformal educational facilities available at times when it is convenient for the children to attend.[25] How do we go about understanding the challenging realities that affect many members of the community, and how do we understand the appropriate steps that are required for this? An example of this can be found in the Idea Box below.

....

25   This can also help to maintain interest in education and preserve the continuity of the educational program.

Facilitating School Attendance

This exercise is very simple to conduct using the Ten-Seed Technique (TST)[26] and should take place at a meeting with community elders.

First, ask the elders to divide the seeds into two groups to represent children who do attend school regularly and children who do not attend school regularly. Next, ask the group how to increase the number of children who attend school regularly. Steer the discussions clear of generalizations, and ask for specific reasons why some children cannot attend. Then, discuss specific ways in which the challenges can be overcome. By the end of the discussions, you might end up with a chart like this:

Attendance Status	Proportion	Reasons for Not Attending Regularly	Suggested Actions for the Community
children attending school regularly		None	Keep encouraging children to attend
children not attending school regularly		Children have to work to help parents	Find out from community how to increase their earning capacity
		Families are unable to provide school uniforms	Provide school uniform support for poor children
		Parents do not consider schooling essential	Make special efforts to convince parents of the value of education

If interim arrangements, such as the provision of school uniforms (or books or fees) are involved, then also work out with the group ways by which these arrangements will be monitored. Ensure that a time limit is set, and avoid making roles and arrangements permanent.

....

26   See details and methodology for the Ten-Seed Technique in my book, *Participatory Poverty Alleviation and Development.*

> When you come across parents who do not see the value of education, it is very useful to try and work at changing this attitude. This can be done through an exposure trip. Taking parents to a new location and giving them the opportunity to hear the stories of transformation from people who once lived in similar situations but have now broken out of their restrictive poverty to develop businesses and careers can strongly influence parents' feelings about education. When I have searched, I have always found such people. More often than not, they are willing to come and share their stories, and sometimes, this is the only way to revive hope in the hearts of parents for better futures for their children. *Persistent poverty can cripple hope or even snuff it out completely. We can help to rekindle it.*

One way to understand contextual predeterminants has been suggested above. Other ways that have been used quite successfully are through realistic movies that are based on the issue. One such movie that had considerable impact in China and elsewhere was a movie produced by the famous producer Zhang Yimou entitled, "Not One Less."[27] This movie has been shown extensively in China and elsewhere around the world and had a very inspiring effect on people. It also mobilized a great deal of support for improving educational facilities in remote areas. Another similar movie, also produced by Yimou, is called, "The Road Home." It tells the story of the strong mobilizing impact that a community can have in creating an educational facility, even in a poor and remote community. In India, several television series have had a powerful influence, especially in inspiring girls to aspire to greater things in life than were ever possible for their mothers.[28] The scope for creativity is extensive, and resources are by no means limited. All one has to do is search and find out what can be appropriately used.

In a later lesson, the use of drama is described.[29] This, too, is a powerful way of reviving hope. Another section explains how to find out the hopes of children and describes exercises that can be used to create opportunities for children to meet with professionals whom they admire, so that the children can

....

27 See http://www.culturevulture.net/Movies/NotOneLess.htm.
28 One of these was originally produced in Japanese, then dubbed over in Hindi. The other was called "Udaan," meaning flight.
29 See section 1, lesson 6.

develop ideas, hopes, and dreams.[30] The professionals can serve as models for the children to aspire to. Success depends on understanding contexts clearly, and then finding a viable solution to overcome the restricting influences of those contexts.

The Cumulative Impact of Prior Negligence

With so many people in need and more being born every day, countries have to prioritize where they will place the emphasis of their development programs. This often results in some regions, sectors, or people groups getting a lower priority for focus than they deserve. As time passes, the *status quo* persists and the circumstances of the overlooked continue to deteriorate. Their circumstances often move from bad to worse, and the limits of community resilience are reached. At this point, the community may begin to turn inward against itself and destroy everything that held it together.

I call this the point where the regressive process becomes self-destructive. There is a limit to the resilience of any community, and when this threshold is crossed, the community begins to lose its identity and the safe confines of its cohesiveness. The result is that the community either breaks up or regresses further into isolation, trying to withdraw from all that might influence it. Future perspective is lost and decisions are taken with very limited foresight. It almost goes without saying that the biggest victims in the process are children.

The circumstances of such communities will continue to deteriorate until some social activists come forward and highlight their cause. As people concerned about child-focused development, it is also our task to continuously search for neglected groups and bring their needs to the attention of the lawmakers, development agencies, and others before the communities reach the limits of their resilience. Just as violence can leave people physically maimed, extreme neglect and poverty can leave people psychologically, emotionally, educationally, or socially maimed for life. When communities reach the point of collapse, large amounts of time, effort, and funding are required to bring them to recovery or self-sustainability.

....
30   See exercises 27, 28, and 29.

Lack of "Booster Support" at Lower HHFSS Levels

As was mentioned previously, families who are at lower levels of Household Food Security Status (HHFSS) require special booster support to develop and maintain economic stability. As families fall to lower levels in the HHFSS scale, they become victims of an exploitative system in the community that bears down on them and saps them of their earning capacity. Not only do they stop being producers, but they also completely lose control of the productive resources in the community. Ironically, even though they now become the service providers, they actually receive fewer social and development services. Prolonged neglect and lack of services cause them to face more and more challenges.

Lack of Ongoing Support for the Extremely Vulnerable Marginalized

Globally, as the number of extremely vulnerable marginalized people grows, it becomes harder and harder to find special funding to cater to their specific needs. We have seen in the HHFSS how those below the charity line require special attention. War victims, victims of major disasters, the elderly, orphans, the disabled, the extremely poor, and those affected by HIV and AIDS also fall into the category of the extremely vulnerably marginalized. Once people fall into this category, helping them requires large amounts of resources and intensive care. Every safety net has to be set in place again to help them stand on their feet once more. This is costly. In fact, some so-called modern development thinking opposes this type of ongoing support, claiming that people who are unable to contribute part of the resources for development ought to be excluded from the development process.

However, good development must consider all groups and make special provisions so that the extremely vulnerable marginalized can receive special ongoing support to catch up with the rest. This applies especially to their children, who are likely to be permanently affected educationally, physically, and socially if this special ongoing support is not provided.

REMOTE LOCATIONS AND MINORITY PEOPLE GROUPS

Rural environments can be far more stimulating than urban ones, and educators can use creativity to offset some of the disadvantages that rural children have in conventional educational models compared to their urban counterparts. Child development experts also emphasize that understanding children properly is an essential part of facilitating quality education. Educators, families, and caregivers need to understand how children grow and recognize that each child learns differently (and that learning styles are also often dependent on the child's learning readiness). It is obvious that this understanding can come from entering into the child's world.

Unfortunately, the education systems in many marginalized rural areas are still far from being ready to meet the challenges of this task. Here, then, is an excellent opportunity for NGOs to play a supplementary role, facilitating the availability of these perspectives to the community so that changes can be initiated and demonstrated. The NGOs can then take these examples and use them to influence policy decisions by advocating for change at the community, provincial or state, and national levels. Much work is needed in this area, and much good can result—the sky is the limit!

All people in a country must be treated with equality. Those that have suffered from isolation and marginalization may need special care to bring them up to speed with the rest of the country. This special provision may be in the form of subsidies, concessions, special educational scholarships, special incentives, special allowances, and so on. Some countries have provisions in their development budgets to meet the special needs of those communities that are located in remote places and for those communities that belong to minority people groups. These special provisions cover the additional costs involved in providing services and support to them, including providing for additional support to those development professionals who have to relocate from their comfort zones to the new areas to work. If countries are not doing this already, they should visit and study countries that are doing it and adopt similar practices.

Failure to Address New Poverty Issues

This is related to the previous cause that was just mentioned. Continued isolation and neglect often force people from remote and minority communities to migrate to urban areas just to survive. People are drawn out of the safe confines of their known and understood culture zones to new, unknown cities. In doing this, the people move from extreme isolation to extreme exposure, and as they try to cope with their new environments, they often encounter severe cultural shock. Since they are unprepared to cope with this, the only way that many people feel that they can cope is to discard their old ways and pick up new ones, thereby losing their cultural anchors.

There is a rapid transition in values, with major decisions being made just to survive. In developing countries, it is not unusual to see some of the ethnic groups still wearing their traditional garb, and involved in labor work such as road or dam construction. Pretty soon, they end up with labor contractors,

moving from site to site in pursuit of labor opportunities. This becomes their new way of life, and all old culture and traditions are discarded. Their children's lives are completely disrupted, and in many cases, the children do not attend school, spend most of their days on the streets, and join the labor force (as child laborers) as soon as they are old enough to start working. They may lose all memories of their previous way of life and the culture they came from.

Culture is an important part of the development process, and it is important to preserve the richness of cultural diversity by providing development opportunities for communities within the safe confines of their own culture.

Loss of Interest in the Parent Generation's Vocation

In my early days of working in rural communities in India, I often came across very strong views and resistance from farmers when I encouraged them to keep their children in school beyond the elementary level. The views they had were that when children went beyond elementary education, their ways and expectations changed. They no longer remained interested in working in the fields or looking after animals. Other parents had had bad experiences too, when they sent their children to secondary school.

What they discovered was that their children had become too sophisticated to want to go back into farming, but were not qualified enough to get other jobs. Thus, they became a generation of misfits in their society, young people who were angry and rebellious. These were often the first recruits of politicians who sought to create any social upheaval in the society. The young people were angry and frustrated enough with life that they were easily persuaded to join anyone who promised to bring revolutionary change. They were also the first to turn to antisocial activities in the area, and remained permanent and prominent examples—"That is what happens to children who get educated."

In several communities, the problems continued for some time until we were able to find ways to help the young people become self-employed, and it also gave us a warning on how not to make the same mistake with future generations. We had the opportunity to participate in the design and implementation of a massive literacy program, ensuring that the curriculum was designed in such a way as to be relevant to the rural needs, providing knowledge and information that was relevant to that part of the country. We also became pragmatic enough to realize that a good number of village youth would not be able to cope with higher education or compete with urban youth for jobs, so we kept the focus on vocational training, working to pass on skills that would enable young people to be self-employed. This is an important aspect to be considered when working with communities.

Perhaps it is now time for development professionals to look more care-fully at the whole issue of education and curriculum development. We need to pragmatically recognize that there is great divide between urban and rural young people and that a balance has to be considered when developing educational programs so that all are educated, including those who may eventually migrate to the cities and those who will remain in the villages.

* * *

Lesson 5:
UNDERSTANDING REALITIES: CULTURE AND PREVAILING SOCIETAL ATTITUDES

ATTITUDE CHANGES HAVE an enormous impact on people. In many of the training programs related to development programming that I facilitate, I make this the theme. The concept of attitude change also applies to the way children are treated by the older generations. It is required to understand the world of children—their needs, their hopes, and their aspirations. It is also needed to ensure that children receive equal opportunities for growth and development.

Culture plays an important role in shaping attitudes, and in either encouraging or hindering attitude change. Culture is the patent that ensures the continuance of a practice. Often, many unhealthy, culture-imposed assumptions continue in communities, hindering positive changes. Culture becomes deeply embedded in people's attitudes, and often, the younger generations are adversely affected by negative preconceived notions within society. Women—and particularly girl children—are often the most affected by these prevailing attitudes, which play a powerful role in dictating what they can and cannot do. Any change is viewed with suspicion and as a threat to the culture; change is therefore strongly resisted. Thus, attitude-related issues must be handled with the greatest of caution, understanding, and patience. There are many examples where this has been done and great things have been achieved. Though the process may be slow, the strategy is appropriate.

Within each culture are community coping mechanisms—ways that communities deal with change and stress but still maintain their group identity. Modernization, globalization, and development, however, have created more changes and stress in many communities than perhaps ever before. Many communities are already stretched to the limit of their resilience and their ability to cope.

Our role, then, can be to help communities to see the gap between their culture and previous ways of life and the new ways of life growing out of modernization, globalization, and development. Communities can then adapt without external imposition. As outsiders, it is hard for us to understand the full significance of a practice or its purpose, so our role often is to widen the horizons of perception, to stimulate appropriate responses. I remember how as a young enthusiastic development worker, I foolishly lectured a villager. I was on a visit to a remote village in India, and discovered, to my utter dismay, that one of the villagers I knew was marrying off his nine-year-old daughter! Thinking back on the incident, I could kick myself for my utter insensitivity and naïveté. All I could think about was how he was breaking the law by giving his underage daughter in marriage. The villager stood silently before me hanging his head down.

Later in the evening after the wedding, he came to visit our campsite and talk with me. It was obvious that he was under the influence of alcohol as he related to me the reality of his world. "You scolded me this morning for marrying off my underage daughter," he said with emotion. "Obviously, you don't know what happens here in the village." The sadness in his eyes compelled me to listen, as he recounted how the rich landlord in the village wielded so much power that when a girl in the village came of age, he demanded that he should have his way with her! Once this happened, there would be no chance of ever getting that girl married into a decent family. Parents thus "chose" to give their daughters in marriage well before they came of age. I grew many years in wisdom and sensitivity that day. As you listen to people in various communities, seek to truly understand how complex their situations are. You will learn to understand many things, especially about societal attitudes and specific community preferences and practices.

One example of a community preference and practice is the preference for a male child, or the practice of continuing to educate only the male child while withdrawing the female child from school. The decision may have been taken after careful consideration and in line with a societal attitude. However, this may be because of a specific existing condition from the past that is no longer valid. Change in the community's attitude, therefore, will have to be preceded by the community carefully reconsidering the changed circumstances to make the appropriate change.

This calls for the role of a change agent. For example, in one country where I worked, a specific conservative community had very strong predetermined career roles for boys and girls. Girls in this society were not to be taught by male teachers beyond a certain age. Thus, despite all the efforts of the social workers in the area, girls were being pulled out of school after a certain age and made to be confined to domestic work, despite the fact that many were doing far better than the boys in their studies. The continued efforts of the social workers did not bear any fruit, and school attendance for girls continued to be nil beyond certain classes.

Not being ones to give up easily, the social workers carried out a situation analysis exercise.[31] They used participatory tools to identify the children going to school and separated the information by gender to show how the girls were actually performing better than the boys up to the point when they were pulled out of school. In the ensuing discussion with the community, several issues came out. This community had strong feelings about girls continuing their education after a certain age. It came to light that this was because there were no female teachers from that same community to teach the girls, and the parents were absolutely against allowing males to teach their daughters.

A vicious circle was thus identified. There were no female teachers, so the girls could not study. Since girls from that community were not continuing studies beyond a certain stage, there would not be any female teachers in future, either! For their parts, the parents were ready to send their daughters to school if female teachers from their community could be found. Thus began a massive search for female teachers from that particular community, resulting in the identification of some who were ready to go into university, but were struggling to find support. A special project was designed for this, and female students from this community were identified and offered scholarships to go to university if they agreed to return to their community as teachers.

Though it took a number of years, girls were now being educated. Some of the students used every vacation to go back to the village school and teach classes such as special season classes. When the university students graduated, they moved back to the village and became full-time teachers. Soon, the scope

....

31   Please see exercises 1–6 for a description of several participatory tools that can be used for carrying out a situation analysis (including gender analysis) for discussions.

of the project was expanded to provide scholarships for men and women from other communities as well. All they were required to do upon completion of their courses was to promise to return to the village to teach for two years. A steady stream of volunteers was created for the organization, and a serious impediment overcome.

A societal attitude is regressive if it restricts opportunities for anyone. However, in this apparent restriction, there may be a built-in protection mechanism that we as outsiders may have failed to note. We must be open to dialogue and sensitive to the reasons that the community has certain attitudes. We must expand our own horizons of perception, and practice a lot of patience and perseverance.

* * *

Lesson 6:
PREPARING AND EQUIPPING
OURSELVES

BOTH THE FACILITATORS and the community must be adequately prepared before children's participation can be mobilized effectively. As we have seen, it would not be helpful to involve children only as tokens or decorations, and it would not be beneficial to the community to allow children's participation only out of a sense of obligation.

Preparing and equipping ourselves for effectively involving children in the process of development is just as important as preparing the community. Facilitators must try to read, learn, and experience as much as possible to prepare themselves.[32] After all, if the facilitators are not convinced about the validity of this approach, or if they do not believe in its potential from the depth of their hearts, how will they influence the community?

Reading stories or, if possible, visiting projects where children's participation is a way of life can be both educational and encouraging. However, the greatest strength will come from actually having been personally involved. I strongly recommend that you try out some of the exercises from this book and determine for yourself that it is something that works. The following preparations are important as we prepare ourselves:

CORRECT ATTITUDE AND WILLINGNESS TO LEARN

This is mandatory. An attitude that is conducive to learning is one that is ready to *listen, be open*, and *see things differently*. First, we have to be convinced that we need to listen to children. When this happens, we will find it very easy to understand the different techniques involved in encouraging children to

....
32   See appendix A for a list of books and other resources that can be consulted.

share their perspectives on various issues. Also, when children begin to share, we will be willing to see things in new ways, and we will be open to their ideas and views. Until we have seen for ourselves that the approach works, it is almost essential that by faith we keep ourselves open, ready to listen, and willing to see things differently!

KNOWLEDGE ABOUT SOME OF THE BASICS OF WORKING WITH CHILDREN

Transitioning from being a person who is used to interacting only with the adult population of a community to a being person who partners with children is not easy. This requires a little reading up and perhaps a visit to the local elementary school and interaction with the teachers on some of the approaches they have in dealing with children. Several important principles are as follows:

- *Keep things simple.* The techniques designed for use with children have to be simple and straightforward, and you must be able to explain them in brief and clear ways. The techniques mentioned and described in this manual are prepared with this principle in mind.
- *Keep things short.* The time spent with children must also be kept brief, because their attention span is short and if the interaction continues for too long, they will lose interest. If several bits of information have to be collected from children, then these exercises must be spaced out with time for games in between to break the monotony.
- *Keep things interesting.* Childhood is a time for fun and laughter, and nothing holds the attention of children better than if it is interesting. Use games and various activities to keep the process interesting. Have some colorful picture books available for the children to read, and make provision for some time of rest.
- *Make it enjoyable.* When these times of interaction are fun-filled and enjoyable, they will guarantee a very high quality of information. This also means that adequate time should be set aside for collecting the information. Usually, the information can be

collected over several days so that the children get enough time to play and have fun in between. This type of activity cannot be rushed or compressed into a short period, so always couple it with other activities that need to be done in the community.

- *Ensure follow-up on issues pointed out by children.* It is important to show children that information provided by them, especially related to things that need to be corrected, is immediately acted upon by the adults. This will confirm to them that we are serious about what we say and will further increase their involvement and enthusiasm.

- *Be positive and focus on strengths.* In your interactions with children, keep the focus positive and appreciative, focusing on the strengths that children have. This should not be a way of telling the children off regarding some of their areas of weakness or failure.

- *Create a little red book.* I have spent a lot of time in China and have read with interest Chairman Mao's views on various topics of development. It is important to also slowly develop a similar book of the thoughts of children on various issues. It would be interesting to know their honest opinions about their teachers and parents, the community leadership, the community development plans, the work of the NGOs in their area, and so on. I encourage you to try and prepare such a booklet. I hope someday to develop and prepare one myself!

- *Obtain training in the techniques.* The techniques to be used with children are quite similar to the PRA/PLA techniques used with adults,[33] but with several modifications in the approach. Child protection and the well-being of children should be central in your considerations and in these modifications, and all of the modifications will require proper understanding,

....

33 For more information, see Lisa Howard-Grabman and Gail Snetro, *How to Mobilize Communities for Health and Social Change* (Health Communication Partnership, 2006), http://www.savethechildren.org/publications/; Robert Chambers, Nicole Kenton, and Holly Ashley, eds., *Participatory Learning and Action 50* (London: International Institute for Environment and Development, 2004); Holly Ashley, Nicole Kenton, and Angela Milligan, eds., *Participatory Learning and Action 56* (London: International Institute for Environment and Development, 2007); Ravi Jayakaran, *Participatory Poverty Alleviation and Development.* See also http://www.iied.org/pubs/.

training, and practice. Look at the examples in this book and slowly develop your own manual with a record of the findings of your own efforts. You will soon become an expert in the use of the techniques yourself and will begin to develop a sensitive appreciation for the views of children.

With this preparation, we will be ready to begin to use the techniques mentioned in the following pages of this manual.

THE ROLE OF PLAY IN A CHILD'S LIFE

Play is a very important part of the lives of children. Children need to play so that they can exercise, move around, and enjoy themselves. Even when children are not given time or space to play because they need to work, they often find a way to make their work into a game. Clearly, children need to be able to play.

Play affects both learning and development. When the use of play is incorporated into the learning process, children learn very quickly. Many effective educational programs use play extensively.[34]

In addition, play affects several areas of a child's physical, cognitive (brain), and social development.

Playing helps children to exercise their muscles, grow stronger, learn to balance, handle small things with their fingers, use many different large and small muscles, and more. The option of play can revive a child who otherwise might have become bored and exhausted. Except when they are sick, children are almost never too tired to play!

Playing also helps children's brain development by helping them to practice reorganizing, regrouping, rethinking, and restructuring information. All of these skills are very important for learning in school and for working in different jobs later in life. Another important form of play is pretending, or

....

34 For example, many schools accredited by the International Baccalaureate use the Primary Years Programme, which emphasizes learning through action, creativity, and an outcomes-based mode of enquiry system. For more on this program, see http://www.ibo.org/pyp/index.cfm.

dramatic play. This helps children to develop their imaginations, to improvise and innovate, and to use local resources.

THE USE OF DRAMA IN DEVELOPMENT WORK WITH CHILDREN

There are few things as powerful as the use of drama while working with children. Drama can be used for a number of purposes, including:

1. *sharing new information* in a creative way;
2. *making information relevant* to the context;
3. *setting the stage for discussions* on an issue;
4. *including children* who are less able to express their thoughts verbally or in writing;
5. *finding out the children's views* on particular issues; and
6. *dealing with sensitive issues* that the children face.

This short list of the potential uses of drama is by no means complete. Hopefully, this manual will encourage you and your colleagues to find new and more innovative ways to use drama based on the principles discussed and the examples shared here. Below are a few tips as you move forward.

Start with a fun activity like a game or group song. This can help the children to overcome any initial shyness that they may feel. Then, describe the situation to be portrayed through the short drama or skit. Ask the children to decide on who the principle characters should be and list these on a board or large sheet of paper. Next, give the group time to ask questions and then ask volunteers to play the key roles. If no children volunteer immediately, ask them to nominate their peers for the roles. After the main characters are assigned their roles, assign some minor roles to others who volunteered but did not get a chance. You can assign the rest of the group to serve as additional minor characters, members of the audience, and judges (one or two children) to assess how well the people play their roles.

Repeat the details of the plot or the issue to be portrayed and then give the children about ten minutes to plan what they will do and say, and how they will act the scene out. If possible, use a video device to capture the skit or drama, and then play it back for them afterward so that they can observe their performance.

On one particular day, our team used drama with a group of child domestic workers. Our goal was to understand and discuss sensitive issues with the children, like the types of violence that they encountered on a daily basis. We chose a common situation—their daily routine—and built a story into it. One of the children was to play the role of a child domestic worker who, in the course of her work that day, had damaged the homeowner's favorite shirt while ironing it. She and others were to depict the reaction of the owner upon returning home and finding out what had happened. The first time through the skit, the children gave a very "sanitized" version of the situation. The homeowner said, "So, you burnt my best shirt? Well, be careful next time." There was a lot of laughter after this portrayal, but when the group was asked if that response showed what would usually happen, there was a resounding "No!"

Once again, the group acted out the same scenario, but this time, we asked a very vocal child to play the part of the owner. She did so, and depicted the violence and abuse that many children experienced daily as she lashed out at the child. At the end of the skit, we sat among the children and asked if the last depiction was more like what they had experienced in their real lives. There were nods all around and many of the children raised their hands, asking for a chance to speak. What followed were heart-wrenching stories of times when they had been victims of abuse and violence.

The session ended with discussion about this, along with their rights as children. They were shown what they should do in situations like this, including how to use a phone and call a helpline. They were also introduced to social workers in their region whom they could contact for help, and assured that the matter would be taken up with concerned authorities in a discreet way where no one would know that they had provided the information.

Today, many educational programs ensure that play is embedded in their curricula for teaching, especially for young children. For example, children are encouraged to develop language and social skills by describing their favorite toys to their classmates as part of their learning. Furthermore, they can learn to negotiate, work together, and share by playing games with other children.

There are, however, several cultural perspectives that underlay each individual's personal definition of and beliefs about play. Some extreme views might actually seek to separate play and learning as though they are unconnected. On the contrary, the best learning often takes place when the learner does not realize that she or he is learning! Therefore, it is essential to properly understand the benefits of play.

Play comes very naturally to children. While many schools for children from wealthy families incorporate play because of their teaching methodologies, many children from poorer families incorporate play into their lives by themselves. They find ways to keep themselves occupied and entertained even in the midst of a heavy schedule of work, squeezing out every available moment to play a game. When the appropriate instruments are not available for playing the game, the children can equally well innovate and find something locally (like seeds, stones, beads, or even small twigs and slippers) that will "make do." Sometimes, the game they are playing may not even  be a well-known one with rules and regulations that have been handed down to them by their friends. If no game exists, a new game is created. If no rules exist, they are made up as the game progresses!

If organizations working with children want to see children develop in a healthy way to their full capacity, then they should seek ways to ensure that this happens through playful learning and playful teaching. They should try to create ample opportunities for children to practice creativity, active games, imagination, learning, language, and social skills through a variety of indoor, outdoor, active, and quiet activities.

In using games, attempts should be made to use local games that the children are used to playing. This has many advantages such as saving on costs (because the games are not resource dependent), using less start-up time (because the children already know the rules and are familiar with how to play the game). Some games, however, require a good deal of imagination on the part of the facilitators to find ways to make the game a learning exercise!

While play in itself is important for children and the use of games can have great impact in the teaching process, there are also several games that can be used for interactively understanding the realities in the lives of children.

This approach is particularly useful with street children, orphans, and other vulnerable groups of children who have experienced trauma. The following games and exercises can be tried out according to the needs and contexts in which these children live.

PROTECTING CHILDREN WHO HAVE EXPERIENCED TRAUMA

For children who have survived traumatic situations such as war, sexual exploitation, or abuse, you will need to take special precautions to make sure that they are adequately protected. For example, you will need to be sensitive to their situations if you ask them to share about their experiences. Sharing can make some children feel sadder, or it can bring back difficult memories. If the children do not wish to share, it may be because of this. Encourage all children in the group to share (do not single out a child or stop them from sharing), but do not keep pushing them to share if they do not wish to do so.

BUILDING AND HOLDING THE INTEREST OF CHILDREN

It is not an easy task to get the attention of children and hold it for a prolonged period. All of us have a limited attention span, and that of children is particularly short. Generally, children's attention spans last for about ten to fifteen minutes (or less for younger children). To effectively encourage their participation, therefore, we need to learn ways to build and hold their attention. The following are some important principles to remember while working with children.

Let Activities Be Hands-On

While interacting with children, ensure that the children get to participate directly. Children enjoy using their hands, feet, and voices. When you plan to perform one of the exercises discussed later in this book, make sure that you plan an opener activity such as a game that will immediately allow the children to actively participate. This will help you to build the children's interest from the beginning. Objects to touch, feel, move, and group will immediately grab their attention, helping you to keep their focus throughout the exercise.

Use Visuals Aids
The topic for discussion or the issue being focused on should be made as visual as possible. Use drawings, photos, diagrams, puppets, or other types of examples that children can see and relate to. This will help them to focus, and it will also activate more parts of their brains, helping them to understand more clearly and remember more fully.

Keep the Children Engaged
When you plan activities, exercises, and discussions, plan to switch gears every ten to fifteen minutes or so. This will help to keep the children interested and engaged in the topic at hand. Here are some ideas for doing this:

- Use variety in the activities, strategies, and teaching methods.
- Be conscious of how short their attention spans are.
- Demonstrate excitement and energy during the time of interaction with them.
- Explain difficult or complicated concepts in simple ways.
- Use role plays, drama, or puppets to convey the message.
- Break into discussion groups that "think, pair, and share."[35]
- Encourage the group to explore and research to find out for themselves by:
  - studying;
  - interviewing;
  - talking and discussing;
  - visiting; and
  - discovering for themselves.

....

35   After an activity such as watching a film or skit or listening to a story, ask the group to first reflect by themselves on what they experienced (think), then to talk about it with a partner (pair), and finally to share it with the larger group (share).

Keep Engagement Relational

It is important to be a people person to work successfully with children. Children, in general, are very relational, and they accept information and engage with new ideas on this basis. Therefore, the facilitator must work in a strongly relational mode, being willing to dedicate time for both individual children and groups of children.[36]

Show Love

Working with children is a special calling and requires people to have a great deal of love and care. Children usually know very quickly which people are genuine, and they often lose interest in interacting with those who do not show them love and affection. Working with children also requires persistent involvement and dedication. If the facilitators do not have this ability, they will probably have very little success in working with children.

1. Let activities be hands on.
2. Use visuals aids.
3. Keep the children engaged.
4. Keep engagement relational.
5. Show love.

BUILDING CONSENSUS WHEN THERE ARE CONFLICTING VIEWS

Sometimes, while children are using participatory methods, they will disagree. It is up to the facilitator and the team to help the children build consensus. There are several ways of working around such situations, but they all depend on the particular context and the circumstances that caused the conflict. Here are some possible alternatives:

....

36   Sadly, the fact that many children are so relational also makes them vulnerable to abuse and exploitation. For example, if a child wants to establish relationships with adults, a pedophile might be able to get them to believe that he or she is trustworthy, and then take advantage of the child. By understanding children's relational nature and meeting them at their point of need, however, we have the opportunity to help them stay safe.

1. If girls' and boys' opinions differ, divide the group according to gender. Record the views for the boys and the girls to share with the larger group later. Perceptions are often different between the two genders, and it can be very helpful to discuss issues with girls and boys separately in order to bring important issues to the forefront.

2. If there are two distinct opinions, divide the group according to those who agree and those who do not. Ask both groups to talk about their observations. Then, bring the larger group back together and ask each group to explain their reasoning and why they believe that their conclusions are different.

You can probably think of many similar ways to handle conflicting views: dividing the group by age, making sure that each child's voice is heard, encouraging the children to listen to one another, and more. Be sure to think through specific scenarios and strategies before you begin the exercises!

The main thing to remember is that you do not need to be afraid of situations where there are conflicting views. In fact, these can often provide for healthy dialogue (as long as there are not any strong emotions involved). A famous person once said, *"You may be right and I might be wrong, but if we listen carefully to each other, we will get closer to the truth!"* This idea opens up so many possibilities: both sides may be right, both sides may be partly right, one side may be right, or both sides may be wrong.

Keep the groups discussing in a positive and open way without getting emotional about it. Then, ask each group to give reasons for their particular stand, remembering to write down all of the points that were raised during the discussion. You will find that often, when the groups listen carefully to each other, both sides become open to the other's perspective and concede to follow a middle path.

Lesson 7:
PREPARING THE TEAM

THIS MANUAL CONTAINS details about many techniques that can be used to encourage and learn from children's participation. You do not have to use every technique in every community or village. Determine in advance the purpose of the intervention and decide on the exercises to be conducted. I have variously referred to the techniques, sometimes as exercises and sometimes as interactions, for that is what they essentially are. In preparing a manual, one of the risks one encounters is that the concepts may be understood as final cut-and-dry methods that have to be followed exactly. This is not the case, and I urge every reader to be flexible and innovative, and feel free to modify and add to the basic techniques that I have described here. In being open and flexible, we learn new things. I hope that in doing this, you will discover new things from the children you seek to work with. Every context is different; hence, the restraining influences in each context are also different. Innovation and flexibility are, therefore, essential. Please read through the techniques with this understanding and you will definitely find them very useful and relevant.

As in my book, *Participatory Poverty Alleviation and Development*, the format I have used here is to first have a definition, followed by a description of the technique, an elaboration of the method, an example of the expected output, and finally, an analysis and discussion related to the technique and its possible application in the programs that you are carrying out. Reading through each  exercise and the details provided will give you a fairly clear idea of how it is to be done and how it works. Ideally, the exercises should be facilitated by someone who has experience in the techniques. If this is not possible,

I suggest you try it out yourself after reading the details to enhance your understanding and build your confidence. The first series of exercises will enable you to collect more general information, and the later exercises will become more focused.

Participatory Rural Appraisal (PRA) and Participatory Learning and Action (PLA) techniques are generally like the examination that a doctor undertakes for a patient. The first few tests are more general, such as looking at the patient's external appearance, taking their temperature, and observing the tongue, throat, and visible mucus membranes. If this does not provide the information required, the doctor will perform more focused examinations such as blood tests or biochemical examinations, or CT scans and X-rays to gain a more specific and detailed profile. Some patients are easier to diagnose simply by virtue of their demeanor, while others require quite a bit of detailed diagnostic probing before their condition can be determined. Try to bear this principle in mind as you explore the worldview of children!

For each of the exercises in the following section, you and your team will need to complete the same initial team preparations. Besides being familiar with the basic essentials by way of attitude and behavior change, it is important to work in teams. Mobilize a Child Participation Mobilization Team to facilitate this initial assessment. This team must consist of at least three people: the facilitator, the documenter, and a team leader. These roles can vary from exercise to exercise and consist of the following responsibilities:

FACILITATOR

This person introduces, explains, and talks the group through the process of the exercise. The *facilitator* must be familiar with how to facilitate and interact with focused groups, and also with some of the basics of reading body language. The team should free up the facilitator to concentrate on the discussion and collect information so that this is done as well as possible. The only writing that the facilitator should do is what appears on the sheet of paper where the discussion is being facilitated. An important principle here is to make this as visual as possible for the participants.

DOCUMENTER

It is very important to faithfully document the essence of the discussion and interaction that takes place during the focused group discussion. The *documenter* sits a little outside the main circle of the focused group discussion and documents the proceedings, listing each point that emerges as a bullet point. Each exercise is documented separately in a bunch of papers (around five to six sheets) stapled together and these are arranged as follows:

1. The first page has details of the name of the exercise, the names of the team members, and the names of the participants in the discussion.
2. The second page has a copy of the final diagram that emerges from the discussions. The documenter should initially leave this blank and copy it only after the discussion is over. The reason for doing this is so that the original can be left behind with the members of the focused group, and also for convenience in documentation for future use.
3. From the third page on, each emerging point of the discussion is documented as a bullet point. All points emerging from the discussion should be noted.
4. After the exercise is over, the facilitator and team leader join the documenter to review all the points discussed and using a highlighter pen to mark the important points.
5. On the last page, a summary is prepared from the important points marked during the discussion.

CHILD PROTECTION IN DOCUMENTATION

To protect each child involved in the activities, you will need to make sure that they know what information you are documenting, how the information will be used, and who it will be shared with. Ask their permission to use the information in these ways. If you are working with issues of abuse or other sensitive issues, you may need to document what is said but not who said it. This can help to protect children from being punished or marginalized because of their experiences. Also, when dealing with sensitive issues, make sure that the group agrees to keep the information confidential (e.g., ask all members not to share specific details from the discussion with others who were not present).

TEAM LEADER

Contrary to expectations, the team leader is not the boss of the team, but the one who serves the other two members by taking care of logistics, ensuring the smooth functioning of the discussion, encouraging those who are not participating to participate, and stopping anyone from disrupting the meeting. The team leader should also be responsible for making sure that child protection issues are planned for and addressed. On occasions when the situation allows, the team leader may pitch in and facilitate a case study, too.

This team of three is expected to work together with their roles being interchangeable so that each team member gets to play each of the roles of team leader, facilitator, and documenter at different times. If assignments undertaken by this team are in multiples of three, each member will get an equal opportunity for fulfilling the different roles. If this small team is part of a very large team, then the coordinator of the operation should ensure that over a period of time, all members of the team receive opportunities to experience each of the techniques described.

DOCUMENTATION AND MAINTAINING RECORDS

As mentioned previously, it is essential to accurately document and record information from the exercises. While this is mainly the role of the documenter, the entire facilitation team should understand the process in order to make sure that the important pieces of information are written down and in order to capture the essence of the discussions for future reference.

HOW TO DOCUMENT EACH EXERCISE

The documentation for each exercise should have the following parts:

1. *Page 1*: the exercise code, names of people who participated, and a list of guiding questions for the exercise;
2. *Page 2*: a drawing or photo of all visuals that were created during the exercise;
3. *Page 3 and following*: transcripts of the discussions with important points highlighted; and
4. *Last page*: a brief summary of the important points.

Whenever you and your team plan a series of exercises, make sure to consider the local context, and make sure that the exercises are relevant for the community that you are focusing on. After you select the exercises, list them in order and give a code to each one (e.g., MCP-01, and so on). This will help in systematically documenting the information.

Determine a set of guiding questions for each exercise. It may be helpful to pilot the questions by trying them out with a few groups and then adjusting as needed. The discussion questions should be relevant to the community, written in simple language, and helpful in finding out the information that you desire. These can be listed on the first page of your documentation.

While the facilitator is facilitating the group discussion, the documenter will write notes (as bullet points) of all the important points that emerge. At the end of the discussion, the documenter will also draw a copy of any charts, diagrams, or other visuals that are created. These pieces of information can be placed on the second and subsequent pages of your documentation.

At the end of the day, the facilitation team should look at the exercises that have been completed and read through the documentation, highlighting the important points. This can help to make the information clearer and avoid repetition. Together, the facilitation team should write the highlighted points into a one- or two-paragraph summary.

Given below is a diagram that shows how the documentation for each exercise can be done:

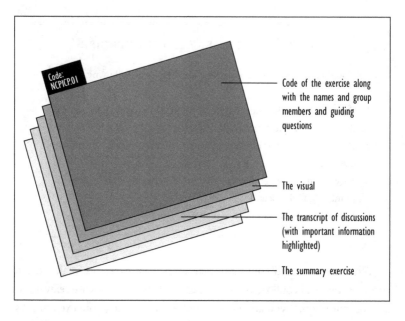

The summaries of each of the exercises (written in order) will make up the community or village summary, which can be used in future activities and discussions.

I recommend leaving the original papers, charts, and other visuals with the village or community so that the participants can continue to refer to them when they need to. Your documentation should be filed in a safe location at your main office. This way, it can be used to brainstorm for future exercises, to prepare for deeper discussions, and to remember the desires and emphases of the children.

Special Safeguards

Earlier, you learned that understanding the realities that children live in can help you to develop specific strategies and plans for your work with them. In addition to this, you will also need to develop special safeguards to protect the most vulnerable children because sometimes, children may be punished, marginalized, or stigmatized because of the things that they share.[37]

Who are the most vulnerable in the community where you work? You will need to determine this based on various factors such as:

- age;
- gender;
- ethnicity;
- abilities or disabilities;
- food security and income;
- living situation; and
- context and culture.

Age

Depending on the circumstances, age can strongly affect a child's vulnerability. For example, in certain parts of Africa, some people believe that having sex with a virgin can cure AIDS. This places younger children at higher risk because they are considered as more likely to be virgins. In other parts of the world, younger children are at higher risk of being trafficked and exploited. Older children often have higher risks of disease and injury because they are more likely to be working and more likely to be sexually active. For your community, consider what different types of experiences children of various ages experience. What types of activities place make them vulnerable to exploitation? Do younger and older children experience different levels of risk?

Gender

Across the globe, boy children and girl children have different life experiences and different vulnerabilities. In many countries, there is a level of discrimination within families that favors boys over girls. This stems from various beliefs

....
37   For more information on child protection, please visit http://www.keepingchildrensafe.org.uk/.

related to the future value of the child.[38] In some Asian cultures, for example, the girl is seen as a child who will ultimately leave the family and become part of her husband's family, while the boy is seen as the one who will remain to look after his parents in their old age. Many religious and cultural practices also reinforce this belief and things keep happening under the guise that "it is the way things have always been." These practices often affect the type of care and nurture that children receive as they grow up. If money for school fees and accessories is scarce, the boy child continues to go to school while the girl child is withdrawn from school. Similarly, if money for good nutritious food is scarce, the girls of the family bear the brunt of the shortfall.

Merely talking about this is inadequate; the issue has to be addressed and your team and the community need to become convinced of the need to treat both genders equally, and possibly even provide extra services for girls if they need help to catch up in areas such as nutrition, education, job skills, and more.

In order to understand the situation in the community, you can hold a series of focused group discussions with groups of girls and boys.[39] This is a situation in which drama has worked well, as well as movies in the local language that tell stories of how girls have excelled.[40] Observe carefully, and ask the children and adults: How are the experiences of boys and girls different in this community? What are boys more at risk of? What are girls more at risk of?

Ethnicity

Ethnic differences can also affect how vulnerable children are. In some places, members of ethnic minority groups are less likely to have their births registered. This can place them at higher risk of exploitation, trafficking across borders, and more. In some countries, there is conflict between ethnic groups, or discrimination against certain ethnic groups.

Try to find out what the ethnic makeup of the community is, and how that affects the children. Are all the children from the same ethnic group? Do

....

38   For more on this topic, see Phyllis Kilbourn, ed., *Shaping the Future: Girls and Our Destiny* (Pasadena, CA: William Carey Library, 2008).

39   See exercises 4 and 11.

40   For example, in India, a number of movies and serials had quite an impact. One very powerful example is a cartoon movie entitled *Mulan*, DVD and VHS, directed by Tony Bancroft and Barry Cook (Orlando, FL: Walt Disney Feature Animation, 1998).

they come from a minority ethnic group? What risks might they face because of their ethnicity?

Abilities or Disabilities

Abilities and disabilities drastically affect individual children and their families. Sometimes, the impact on the family is so serious that it moves them down into a different household food security status level. This is because the family essentially loses one earning member as one spouse now has to stay home and take care of the disabled child. Often, negative attitudes toward disabled children affect the children and their families, and can even cause their basic rights to be denied.

In addition, few organizations provide special programs for disabled children. However, I have observed that in almost every community-initiated development plan, communities have requested special provisions for families with disabled children.

It is also important to remember that this is labor-intensive work, and the staff needs special skills and an especially caring heart. It is beyond the scope of this book to go into details of all the different types of special care required. It is, however, necessary to carry out a disability survey in the community to identify how many children have special needs.

A DISABILITY SURVEY

In order to find out how many children with special needs live in a community, you can perform a disability survey using the Ten-Seed Technique (TST). Gather the village elders and explain that ten seeds will represent all of the children in their community. Ask them to distribute the ten seeds into two groups, one group for nondisabled children and one for disabled children. In one community, the elders identified that around 5 percent of the children among them (half of one seed) had some type of disability.

Rapid Disability Survey			
Children with disabilities			
Minor physical abnormalities	Major physical abnormalities	Mental abnormalities	Blindness
● ● ● ● ● ●	● ● ●	●	●

In the second stage of the exercise, explain to the elders that now, you will be using the ten seeds to represent only the disabled children. Ask the group to classify the seeds according to the types of disabilities that exist (see figure above).

Facilitate a discussion about these topics. How can the community help these children and their families? What types of programs would the affected families benefit from? What do disabled children have to say?[41]

Small centers where a staff person can give advice to caretakers on topics such as how to help develop the muscles and how to teach basic literacy have been very helpful in many communities.[42] In the case of the community where the disabled children were identified (see sidebar above), the NGO held special training sessions for the caretakers (mostly mothers and older female siblings) on how to look after the children, give them a massage, and exercise their muscles. The NGO also held functional literacy classes for the children and encouraged the community to include the disabled children in the community school. Prior to sending the children to the school, the NGO

....

41   For more on mobilizing the participation of disabled children, please see Save the Children, *Learning to Listen: Consulting Children and Young People with Disabilities* (London: Save the Children, n.d.), http://www.childinfo.org/files/childdisability_SavetheChildren.pdf.

42   See Sandy Neimann, Devorah Greenstein, and Darlena David, *Helping Children Who Are Deaf: Family and Community Support for Children Who Do Not Hear Well* (Berkeley, CA: Hesperian Foundation, 2004); Sandy Niemann and Namita Jacob, *Helping Children Who Are Blind: Family and Community Support for Children with Vision Problems* (Berkeley, CA: Hesperian Foundation, 2000); and David Werner, *Disabled Village Children: A Guide for Community Health Workers, Rehabilitation Workers, and Families* (Berkeley, CA: Hesperian Foundation, 2006).

held special classes for the nondisabled children to be sensitive and support these children when they struggled to keep up with the rest.

Food Security and Income

We have seen that household food security status affects every aspect of the lives of people in a community. As a family moves to higher levels of food security status, they gain more access to the various services available in the community. Their personal wealth (both assets and available money) gives them greater access to loans, moneymaking opportunities, hired employees, land, and more.[43] These multi-pronged accesses ultimately also give them greater access to machines, technology, and other items (physical capital) in their area that can help them to further improve their household food security status. In other words, the stronger the family's food security, the more options and access the family has. This complex and subtle process of "capture and exclusion" can be seen in almost every community around the world.

Sometimes, even the assets created especially for the extremely poor, such as schools, medical clinics, and other facilities, stay out of their reach. Just because it is within walking distance does not mean that all children have equal access.

For example, on one trip to Myanmar, a team and I were walking down the street of a village when we came across some children playing house. As we stood and talked with the children, they described the various items of food they were cooking in their make-believe game. This was how the children often spent their free time between returning from school and waiting for their respective mothers to call them back home for dinner. There was joy on their faces and much laughter as they pretended to cook.

Less than five feet away from these joyful children sat another child of the same age. This child, however, was selling snacks to supplement his parent's meager income. The contrast was very clearly visible: for some children, cooking was a fun game, but for others, it was a harsh reality. For the working child, it was not a way to pass the time; it was *real life and survival!* The school was just around the corner from this street, and the development agency in the area had planned for the school based on the number of children in the area. They had even made provisions to ensure that schooling was free for

....

43 The more wealth they have, the more access they gain to financial, social, human, and natural capital.

all children. Nevertheless, the fact that this child had to work stopped him from attending the school.

> While we try to create equal opportunities for all the children in the community, we also need to ensure that special safeguards are in place to ensure that no groups of children get excluded from gaining access and thus benefiting from the program. These safeguards can be determined through monitoring the level of access (as in this case of school access for all) after the program has been put in place. You can also ask a focus group of children about how many children are still unable to go to school, and you can facilitate a discussion with both children and adults about what measures need to be put in place to ensure that all children can go to school. This may then entail the introduction of special scholarships for some children or a compensatory income generation program for some of the parents. It requires a lot of flexibility in our program for appropriate adaptation, but the results will be well worth the effort.

Clearly, the food security status and income of a family strongly impact the opportunities of the children. Because of this, it is important to develop special safeguards for children with less access to food and income and to help families gain opportunities and training to improve their situations.

Living Situation

One of the most well-known examples of a living situation that affects children's lives is that of children who work or live on the streets. It is not always easy to determine exactly what the number of street children[44] in a country is, but the issue of children living on the streets is a growing problem in almost every developing country. Some street children spend a large part of their time working on the street, but then return home at night to sleep. Others work and live on the street, making their living by themselves and sleeping where they can. While life is harsh for both groups, the second group often has a more difficult situation because they do not have a family to go back to at night, and because they might not have a network of support for when they

....

44 We understand that to some, the term "street children" has negative connotations. For the purposes of this book, however, we have chosen to use the term because it is commonly understood.

become ill or do not have enough food or money. Street children face many harsh realities every day, and their living situation requires special precautions within our programs.

Children who live in slums, refugee camps, unsafe buildings, or other difficult circumstances will also require special considerations because of their living situations. Be aware of certain locations that may feel safe or unsafe to children,[45] routes that children generally take to walk around, and potential dangers within their communities. Encourage the children to share their ideas about locations and strategies that can help make their community a safer place!

Context and Culture

Specific details about a community's history, location, and culture can create the need for special safeguards. For example, a community that is recovering from a recent tsunami or earthquake will have certain needs that other communities might not have. Refugee children, children affected by war, children who live in areas where diseases such as HIV and AIDS are prevalent, and others may be more vulnerable simply because of the current situation of their community. You will need to carefully consider the *context* of the community in order to develop effective strategies.

In addition, different religious views, community rituals, or cultural practices might be harmful to children and might require specialized strategies to empower the children to share their views. These components of *culture* might be deeply ingrained within both the children and adults of the community. For this reason, it is important to not just try to correct people, but rather to give them the information and tools that they need in order to understand why a practice might be harmful to children.[46]

....
45   For more on safe and unsafe places in the community, see exercises 5 and 6.
46   For more information, see www.keepingchildrensafe.org.uk.

Preparing for Safety and Sustainability

It is important to think carefully about safety and sustainability as you prepare for children's participation. Here are a few questions to consider regarding safety:

- What can our team do to make sure that all children are kept safe during our activities?
- How can we make sure that no child is marginalized or stigmatized because of information that is shared?
- How can we make sure that when children share about sensitive subjects, the information is kept confidential?
- What should our team do to protect ourselves from injury and accusations?
- What policies do we have in place for if a child or adult is injured, abused, or accused?[47]

Regarding sustainability, think about these questions:

- What resources and information should we write down for others to use in the future?
- Who should we train in these techniques?
- How many people should we train?
- What types of finances, technology, and other resources are needed to keep doing what we are doing?

....

47   Child protection is very important. For more details, checklists, and training materials, please visit www.keepingchildrensafe.org.uk. Please also see Bill Forbes, *Celebrating Children Workbook 6: Child Protection*. Kerstin Bowsher and Glenn Miles, series editors. Available online at www.viva.org, under "Viva Equip People."

* * *

Lesson 8:
PREPARING THE COMMUNITY

P REPARING THE COMMUNITY to respond appropriately to children's participation is also very important. The first thing that the community needs to be
prepared for is that the participation of children is immensely significant and
valuable in the development process. Often, when organizations transition to
child-focused development and invite children's participation, they pass through
a stage of uncertainty. It is a new dimension and a new approach, so there are
many assumptions regarding what child participation is all about.

Typically, the first changes do not provide the really encourage children's full
participation. When there is heavy donor pressure to make child participation
a part of the project design without strong support and understanding of how
to mobilize children's participation in healthy ways, children may end up being
manipulated into saying or doing what the adults have already predetermined.
Sometimes, their involvement is more in the form of a *decoration*, where they
are visible during the event in the form of a performance, but are not really
part of the entire process.

Tokenism may also occur when children are asked for their opinion just for the
sake of asking, but their opinions are never really taken into consideration. These
options are not considered true participation on the part of the children.

True child participation can vary between the more paternalistic attitudes
of *assigning tasks* for children to perform to *consulting* with children and
informing them of the adults' decisions to truly *consulting* and *collaborating*
with children in making joint decisions.[48] Mobilizing child participation is a
process that organizations have to take time to learn!

We must learn to let go and let children take the lead. This requires quite
a bit of preparation. To begin with, the community must first be convinced
that this is not just a donor requirement that requires some adjustments to the

....
48   Hart, *Children's Participation.*

way we refer to things. They have to first understand that we are convinced that it is a better way of doing business and that the turnaround has special value. The community must be convinced that the plan to have children participating is not a passing fad, but that it is mandatory. This means that time has to be taken with the community to convince them of the benefits by giving concrete examples from places where children's participation has been adopted. This will also improve the quality of the outcome and perhaps, help the community to become a good example for others in the future.

How to Help the Community See the Value of Children's Participation

The following are several ideas that can be useful in convincing the community and preparing it to start a program involving children's participation:

1. Explain how children will benefit. Children have experience and ideas about their needs, hopes, and desires. In listening to children, the community will hear new perspectives and new insights about what is best for children. After all, children are the primary beneficiaries of any long-term strategy.
2. Explain how adults will benefit. Active children's participation frames the way for better relations between the generations in the community. Listening to children will foster better dialogue between the generations and better enable learning and experience to pass from generation to generation.
3. Exercise patience. Convincing requires patience and overcoming old ways of thinking such as the idea that children are to be seen and not heard.
4. Give concrete examples. Concrete examples and outputs of exercises from other communities (and also from the same area) are good ways of convincing a community.
5. Share the broader perspective. Discussions about child participation may be a good way to pass on key community development plans from one generation to the next so that there is better understanding of the purpose and greater ownership by future generations.
6. Be intentional. Explain that involving children is not a passing fad, but that this approach is used intentionally.

7. Value children. Work to help the community realize that investing in the child is investing in the future, and therefore, it is important to recognize that children have a right to determine how that future should look.

A while ago, my team and I carried out Participatory Learning and Action (PLA) exercises in a village in the Yunnan province in the People's Republic of China. We asked a group of farmers to use of the Ten-Seed Technique (TST) to show us what the problems of the children in their village were. The following were the observations of the group:

Problems Faced by Children From the perspective of adults	YUNNAN PROVINCE, PRC
Parents cannot afford to send them to middle school and university	● ● ● ●
Cannot speak 'Puthughwa' (Mandarin) very well	●
Parents unable to provide nutritious food	● ● ●
Keep watching TV, but do not read books	●
Insufficient clothing	●

PLA with children's group RIJ/QPI/WVIC

We shared this information with the larger community and they all agreed that this was indeed the case. A careful observation of this output will show us that the adults perceived the problems of children as being the result of *what they as parents were unable to provide* for their children. Even the inability to speak Mandarin was understood to be a problem that they, as the parent generation, had caused for the children, because of the need for the children to also learn and be proficient in their own minority language. We then tried to find out from the children's group what their perceived problems were. We tried to facilitate the process in a way that the children would best be able to express themselves. They wanted to first show us what made them unhappy:

What Makes Children Unhappy	YUNNAN PROVINCE, PRC
They don't get to sleep well at night	● ●
Being beaten and scolded by parents	● ●
When parents don't buy them the things they want	● ● ●
Getting poor results in school	● ● ●

PLA with children's group RIJ/QPI/WVIC

As we laid out the seeds, we began to discuss with the children the details of what they were telling us through the choice of proportions of seeds. It was interesting to enter their world and understand their situations from their perspectives. The slide above shows what made the children of this particular community unhappy. The children were concerned about their ability to sleep well, about the attitude of their parents toward them, about their results in school, and about not receiving from their parents what they wanted. These were very different from what the adult group perceived as their problems or difficulties. Even the fourth area that children were unhappy about (their school results) was viewed differently by the children and the adults.

The adults thought of poor results as being the result of a lack of responsibility on behalf of the children. The children, however, saw it as something by which they had let their parents down. They had tried hard to do well in school, but it was a struggle. The issue was definitely not one of a lack of responsibility! We persisted further in the exploration of the worldview of the children. They continued to explain this to us by showing us through the use of the TST what they did not like. The following slide shows how they placed the seeds:

What Children Don't Like	YUNNAN PROVINCE, PRC
Don't like fighting and scolding	● ● ● ●● ●
Don't like cutting trees and picking flowers	● ●
Don't like the task of grazing cows	●
Don't like wandering	●

PLA with children's group RIJ/QPI/WVIC

A review of this slide shows that these are largely related to their relations with their parents. The children did not like being scolded or living in an environment where there was quarreling in the house. They did not like people picking flowers or cutting down trees. This was a sharp reminder to us that children are also concerned and aware of environment related issues. The children placed importance on the need to preserve beauty and greenery. Interestingly, too, they disliked the task of grazing animals. They felt this was a waste of time and that they were missing out on opportunities for play or other activities during this time.

The fourth thing they disliked was "wandering around." This seemed strange in the beginning. If they did not like wandering around, then why did they wander around? It was interesting how the layout of seeds provided an interesting visual aid for discussion and dialogue. Whenever adults saw children "doing nothing," they had a tendency to *give them an assignment* to keep them busy. To avoid this, the children often "wandered around" away from where their parents would see them and give them some useless assignment! This sparked off some laughter in the group of facilitators, but the children did not laugh about it as it was a very serious issue for them. For the children, this issue was one where they felt that adults were "unable to understand their situation."

The discussion with children as equals was beginning to bring up really interesting perspectives! As the discussion progressed, we asked them to use the seeds to show us the things that they liked. The following slide shows how they distributed the seeds:

What Children Like	YUNNAN PROVINCE, PRC
Like to go to school	● ● ● ●
Like to do housework (domestic chores)	● ● ●
Like to play	● ●
Like to plant flowers	●

PLA with children's group RIJ/QPI/WVIC

As can be seen from this slide, the children loved going to school and learning, even though it often turned out to be quite a challenge. Contrary to the assumptions of the adults, they loved helping out in the house with

domestic chores, because this gave them a sense importance. Of course, they also loved to play, and we were able to learn a great deal about the different games they played. An interesting thing related to this was that they were particularly frustrated when adults barged in on their game and broke it up when calling them away for a task or for a meal. The children were upset that they were not allowed to finish playing the game that was in progress.

Some children were especially vocal about this, citing examples of times when they were winning a game and it was abruptly ended by an adult intervention. Again, when some of the adults laughed at this, the children maintained serious expressions. It was obviously an issue they felt strongly about! Finally, the children also loved planting flowers. This was common to both the boys and girls, and a finding that can benefit future agricultural and environmental protection activities in the community.

Later, during the corporate community level feedback of the outputs of different exercises, we showed the community first the adult perception of the problems of children. After we had their consent and consensus about this, we showed them what the children's perceptions were. There was silence as the adults looked at the outputs. Some of them looked with surprise at the group of children as they sat by at one side of the room, wondering how they had failed to understand this about their own children. It was obvious that there was a gap between the generations in understanding each other. It was a proud privilege for us to then present them with a technique that was plain, simple, and versatile as a method to help them bridge the gap.

Because the community had actually experienced the results of children's participation and seen how the plan of action was richer as a result, they recognized the value of children's participation and became more willing to listen to the children and incorporate the children's suggestions.

Section Two

EXERCISES

* * *

Exercise 1:
MAP OF THEIR WORLD

Important Places in Our Community

Overview: The "map of their world" exercise is facilitated with children to find out more about the places in the community that hold significance for them. *The purpose of this exercise is to see where the children spend their time, and what places in the community are important and precious to them.*

Children:
- ✔ Girls and Boys
- ✔ 7 to 16 years of age

Supplies:
- ✔ Large sheet of paper
- ✔ Coloring pens or crayons

Method: After building rapport with the children, find a comfortable place for them to work on the map. Provide them with a large sheet of paper and some coloring pens or crayons. Then, ask them to draw the Community Map showing the places that they frequently visit or where they spend a lot of their time. As the diagram starts to form, encourage them to show as many details as possible about the particular locations on the map. While facilitating, try to ensure that each child has an equal opportunity to make a contribution to the creation of the diagram. Ensure that the children have plenty of bright-colored writing pens or crayons to use, and ask them to draw their favorite spots with colors that they like. Later, try to find out the reasons for the special choices of colors. After the diagram is completed, ask questions to ensure that the children did not forget any important places. When this has been confirmed, ask them to take you to each of the locations in the map and compare their drawing of it to the way it really looks. Like all the other exercises, the output from this should also be shared with the larger group.

Expected output: The picture above shows a map created by children in this way. It is very interesting to see that the map of their world often looks like a collage of spots and locations rather than a map. The emphasis is often on the spots themselves rather than the way to get to the spot or the relationships that the spots have with one another.

Analysis and discussion: An analysis of the diagram shows that often, the drawings are quite different from the actual structures. In addition, favorite spots are depicted as being far greater in size than the real structure. Favorite

spots are drawn in colors that children like—usually bright colors like red, green, and blue. Visiting each location and comparing it to the map is also important because one can then continue the discussion with the children to find out why the location is a favorite. Sometimes, the actual place looks very different from the diagram in the map. At other times, something that ought to have been in the diagram is conspicuously absent. This is because the things that are liked are usually depicted bigger than they are, while non-favorite spots are shown very small or ignored completely. It is also surprising that frequently, when the map of their world is shown to the larger group in the feedback session, the other children are able to recognize the locations, while the adults find it difficult to make sense of the map!

OUR COMMUNITY
....

Exercise 2:
TIMELINE

Our Community's History

Overview: The timeline is a profile of the village or community over the past few years, as perceived by a group of children or an individual child.

Description: This is an exercise that can be conducted with a group of children to understand their perspective of the history of the village or community. Because of the way this exercise is conducted, it usually tends to highlight the events that had a strong impact on children, either good or bad. The exercise can also be conducted for individual children to see how their lives were impacted by the events in the context in which they live. The purpose of this exercise is to identify the events that impacted the lives of children in the context in which they live.

Method: Find a location that children are familiar with and where they feel comfortable. This could be a school classroom, a playground, or even a building. Ensure that the surroundings are quiet and nonthreatening and set the right mood for discussions by starting with some games that children enjoy. If the children feel intimidated by the presence of adults from the village, find a way to engage the adults away from the place where the timeline exercise is to be conducted. It is good for the community adults to be visible so the fears of the children are allayed. It is also a good safeguard principle for outsiders. However, try to move the adult group far enough away so that while they can see what is happening, they are out of earshot. When the atmosphere is relaxed, explain the purpose of the exercise. Tell the children (seven to sixteen years old would be best for this exercise) that you want to find out about the interesting things that happened in their village that they remember. Ask them to think back to the time when they were very young and recall the events they remember. As the events are recalled, determine the approximate date and continue to ask them, "What else?"

Continue with this until the current period. The issues recalled will be more in number as you discuss the previous six months or so. Keep track of the information on a large sheet of paper with basic drawings or diagrams of the events. The children will love to make visuals of the events; encouraging them to do this will also make it easier for them to identify the events.

> Similarly to the "river of life" exercise (see exercise 15), this exercise can also be done with individual children, asking them to describe important events in their own lives.

Once the information has been collected and recorded on the paper, ask the children to present their timeline to the group. This will provide opportunities for feedback, changes, and/or agreement. Any corrections or modifications that are required can then be carried out. This process is referred to as *triangulation*, where the information collected from a small group is presented to a larger group to hear more perspectives. Finally, have the group identify one of the participating children who feels confident to make the presentation. Keep the timeline paper and other information to share at a community-level feedback meeting that should be scheduled for a later time when all the planned exercises are completed. Make sure that the names of the group members are written down at one side of the paper for future reference. This is important to do, especially if some clarification is required afterwards.

Expected output: The following example shows how the output of carrying out such an exercise may look:

Approx. Year	Event
1999	Old school roof blew off. School closed for many days.
2000	School shifted to other side of the hill.
2001	Heavy rain and flooding. School closed for many days.
2002	New school block constructed with cemented play space for games. New fish pond constructed.
2003	New enclosure created near school with trees. Old playing enclosure building broken by outsiders. Bridge constructed behind school to cross river during rainy season.
2004	School had big party and very good magic show. School received many pieces of equipment for games. Many friends started studying in different rooms. Water came through pipes from the river. Big television set in village chief's house. Many visitors from foreign countries. Some can sing and dance. Showed film about animals.

Analysis and discussion: An analysis of the timeline above shows that the children were able to recall only the things that *significantly affected their lives.* These were mainly related to the school building, the playground, entertainment, and the flooding that affected their school attendance. They remembered aspects of the enlargement of the school, more because it resulted in some of their friends (who all sat in the same classroom) moving to other classrooms. Similarly, the changes in the places where they played, such as the old dilapidated building, caused them much sadness. Entertainment was also of great importance in what the children remembered. Special programs for celebration, the new television, and the performances by visitors were, therefore, remembered well. The introduction of piped water was also something remembered with a lot of discussion related to the way it had reduced some of the chores they had to share in before going to school. An interesting aspect of this was that the children did not see any difference in the fact that that the water was now filtered at the overhead tank on top of the hill before distribution. It became obvious that no one had explained to the children about this. Some of them, it was discovered, still drank water at the stream on their way to and from school! The fish tank, interestingly, was nothing but the water tank prepared during the construction, which had some small fish in it!

OUR COMMUNITY
....

Exercise 3:
TRENDS ANALYSIS

How Our Community Has Changed

Overview: The trends analysis exercise portrays the changes that have taken place in the lives of children, as perceived by children.

Description: This is an exercise that can be conducted with a group of children to understand their perspective of the changes that have taken place in their village or community during their lifetimes. Here, too, we look at only those aspects of change that the children identify, with the purpose of seeing which subjects they talk about. As in the timeline exercise, children often remember and mention only those things that have impacted their lives, whether positively or negatively. *The purpose of this exercise is to identify the changes that have impacted the lives of children and how the children have adapted to and coped with these changes.*

Method: To carry out this exercise, randomly identify boys and girls between seven and sixteen years old. Make sure to include children from different age groups. Bring them together and play a few games, do a group activity, or use other methods to establish a good rapport with them. Next, explain the exercise. Set a large paper in the center of the group, dividing it into three sections by drawing vertical lines. If you will be using the Ten-Seed Technique (TST) as explained below, divide the paper into five columns.

Ask the children to think back to the time when they were very small, and share with the group what the changes are in the way they live their lives now compared to the past. As they name the changes, ask one of the children to  list these (or draw or diagram them if required). This listing of the past is done in the first column. After the children have mentioned (allow them to do this on their own—without external prompting) all the things that have changed, go back to the first item on the list and ask them to identify how it has changed. Use the second and third columns to write a description of the change. The second column is used to describe how it was in the past and the third column is for identifying the current state. After the information is collected, share it back with the group to ensure that you have understood it clearly and also for triangulation, or feedback from a larger group.

To identify how much change has taken place, you can use the Ten-Seed Technique. Have the children divide up ten seeds between the two categories of "before" and "now" to express their ideas about the extent of the changes that have taken place in their communities.

Expected output: The following example shows how the output from carrying out such an exercise might look:

Type of Change	Extent of Change (TST)		Details of Change	
	Before	**Now**	**Past**	**Present**
Housing	●●● ●●	● ●●●●	Not so comfortable	More comfortable
Transport	● ●	●●● ●●● ●	Most people walked	Many motorcycles and cycles
School Attendance	● ● ●	● ●● ●●● ●	Many of our friends did not go to school	Now most of our friends attend school

Shops in the Community	● ●	● ● ● ● ● ● ● ●	Very few shops sold things for children	Lots of nice things available in the shops
Time for Playing	● ● ● ● ● ● ●	● ● ●	Lots of time to play	Not enough time to play
New Things	● ●	● ● ● ● ● ● ● ●	Very few new things like television or videos	Most families have television and videos
Tasty Food	● ● ● ●	● ● ● ● ● ●	Did not like the food so much	Parents give us many nice things to eat
Activities for Children	● ● ●	● ● ● ● ● ● ●	Very few activities in school	Many interesting activities in school

Analysis and discussion: An analysis of the exercise above shows the types of issues that children recognized as having changed in the past few years. Clearly, many changes took place in the community, and the group of children was able to identify particular changes that had an impact on them. The changes they observed were related to housing, transport, school attendance, shops in the community, time for playing, food, new things, and activities in school. The extent of change is often quite noticeable, and in this exercise, the actual change is only identified in terms of the children's perspectives. There is definitely more emphasis on the changes that children either greatly liked or greatly disliked. This gives us an immediate insight into their world and is useful in understanding how children feel. Another important element to note is that the focus group inadvertently consisted of only school-going children, hence the views of out-of-school children are not reflected. Care must be taken to ensure that the group is well balanced, including some children who are not attending school.

OUR COMMUNITY
....

Exercise 4:
GENDER ANALYSIS

Girls and Boys in Our Community

Overview: The gender analysis exercise is aimed at finding out the different ways in which children of different genders are treated in a community.

Description: This exercise can be conducted with a focus group of children from seven to fifteen years of age. The group must have almost equal numbers of girls and boys. Alternately, the exercise can be conducted with two separate groups, one for boys and one for girls. *The purpose of the exercise is to find out if there is any variation in the treatment of girls and boys. It is also done to see what the children's perspective of this treatment is.*

Method: To carry out this exercise, build rapport with the group and then give the children a large sheet of paper divided into three columns. In the first column, ask the children to list the various criteria to be considered about where the situation is different for boys and girls. In the second and third columns, use ten seeds for each category to illustrate which group (boys or girls) experiences these things more often, or if both boys and girls experience these things equally.

Expected output: The following is an example of this exercise:

Criteria	Boys	Girls
Number of participants under age 16 in the community	61	39
Ratio	• • • • • •	• • • •
Ratio of children in school	• • • • •	• • • • •
Ratio of children not in school	• • • • •	• • • • •
Ratio of children who have dropped out	• • •	• • • • • • •
Have to help with housework at home	• • • •	• • • • • • •
Get more time to play	• • • • • •	• • • • •
Help in the cooking	•	• • • • • • • •
Eat more	• • • • • •	• • •
Leave the village to work	• • •	• • • • • •
Help in the family's agricultural activities	• • • • • • •	• • •
Help in house repair work	• • • • • • • • •	•
Feed animals	• • • • • • •	• •
Carry water	• •	• • • • • • • •
Get more praises from parents	•	• • • • • • •
Get more scolding from parents at home	• • • • • • •	• •
Involved in fighting and quarrels	• • • • • • • •	•
Can earn more money to support parents	• •	• • • • • • •

Analysis and discussion: An analysis of the information collected from the focus group showed the different types of experiences of the girls and boys in the same age groups in a particular village in Cambodia. The total number of children available in the village is also an indicator of the survival strategy of the community in sending children away to work in the homes of families in

the village as child domestic workers. While the ratios of girls and boys in school and out of school are fairly equal for the children who remain in the village, the number of girls available for the exercise is significantly less than the number of boys. In this community, since girls are often able to earn much more than boys, and hence can start contributing to home expenses at a much earlier age, they are often sent away to work at a young age. Both boys and girls are expected to

share in the workload at home, but there is a difference in the types of work that they are expected to do. Boys tend to be more aggressive than girls and their playfulness and naughtiness keeps surfacing, and as a result, they get more scoldings than the girls do. Overall, there is also a clear indication that children in general do not have enough time to be carefree and enjoy life as children. Ironically, these are the ones who are still left in the village, whose lot is much better than those that have left the village to start working to support their families financially. When the information from such exercises is shared with the larger group of children, it is surprising how much they understand what is happening.

OUR COMMUNITY

. . . .

Exercise 5:
SAFETY PROFILE A

The Safe Places in Our Community

Overview: This exercise about the concept of a safe place is conducted to find out from children, especially the most vulnerable children, what they consider to be a safe place.

Description: This exercise is designed to identify the various indicators that vulnerable children, such as street children, describe as ways to recognize a safe place. *The purpose of the exercise is to understand the vulnerable children's perspectives on what is considered to be a safe place.*

Method: With a group of seven- to fifteen-year-old children, build rapport and explain the exercise. Next, ask the children to prepare a map of places that they visit on a regular basis. Have them circle the places that they think are safe places to visit. Help the children to list these safe places across the top of a large sheet of paper. Down the left column, list the reasons why the children consider a place to be safe. After the list is completed, ask the children to rank each location for each of the reasons, using 1 for the safest place and 5 for the least safe place for each row. What we will discover is that, sometimes, even though the children know a place is not safe, they will visit it when they are desperate.

Expected output: The following diagram shows the output generated from such an exercise:[49]

Criteria for considering it safe	List of Five Most Safe Places On the Map				
	Location 1	Location 2	Location 3	Location 4	Location 5
No danger of being robbed	●● ●●	●●● ●●	●	●●	●●●
No danger of being beaten by older children	●●● ●	●●●●	●	●●	●●●
Can relax and sleep without fear	●●● ●	●●●● ●	●	●●	●●●●
A place where we can count our money	●●● ●	●●● ●	●	●●	●●●
A place to freely discuss with friends	●● ●●	●●● ●●	●	●●	●●●
A place to play and be involved with fun activities	●● ●●	●● ●●	●	●●	●●●
A place with nice music	●●●●	●●●●	●	●●	●●●●
A place where we can get something to eat			●	●●	●●●
A place where we can believe what we are told			●●	●	
A place where even those not *Khlang* (strong) can survive, and where children like us are welcome			●		
A place that you consider "most safe"	●●● ●	●●● ●●	●	●●	●●●●

....

49   Note that several of the boxes had to be left empty because the criteria did not apply.

Analysis and discussion: An analysis of the information above showed that this group of children used very clear indicators to determine where they could be safe. Of these, Location 3 (the street children drop-in center and shelter of a non-governmental organization in the area) turned out to be the place that they considered to be the safest. Location 4 was a free clinic for poor children and scored second highest points in order of safety. At a later time, this matrix could be expanded, and the children could be encouraged to outline more indicators of safe places.

The results of this exercise can be used in a number of ways. For example, non-governmental organizations and others can use the information to improve the quality of their services by working on the areas where they scored the least points, thereby making their locations safer places that will attract more of the community's vulnerable children.

* * *

Exercise 6:
SAFETY PROFILE B

The Unsafe Places in Our Community

Overview: This exercise examines the children's concept of unsafe or dangerous places. It is conducted to find out, especially from the vulnerable children,
what they consider to be an unsafe place.

Description: This exercise is designed to learn about the various indicators that
vulnerable children (such as street children) use as being a means to identify
an unsafe place. *The purpose of the exercise is to understand the vulnerable
children's perspective on what is considered to be an unsafe place.*

Method: Like the previous exercise, children are asked to prepare a map. In
this case, ask the children to draw places that they usually try to avoid.[50] After
they have done this, ask them to circle places they think are unsafe to visit.
Using the Ten-Seed Technique (TST), have them place seeds at each of the
locations according to how dangerous they are. This will help to identify the
five or six most unsafe locations.

Next, list these locations along the top of a large sheet of paper. Down
the left side, list the reasons that the children give for considering a place to
be unsafe. After the list is completed, have the children rank each location
....

50 The children might not include certain "unsafe" locations if they never find it necessary to go
there. If you feel that this information is important for you to know, you can either ask questions
about additional locations, or you can continue the exercise later and have the children rank an
additional list of locations.

for each reason given with 1 for the most dangerous place and 5 for the least dangerous place.

Expected output: The following diagram shows the output generated from such an exercise:[51]

Criteria for considering it unsafe	List of Five Most Unsafe Places on the Map				
	Location A	**Location B**	**Location C**	**Location D**	**Location E**
Sudden and unexpected clearance drives by authorities	● ●	●	● ● ●	● ● ● ●	● ● ● ●
Under special observation of the police	● ●	●	● ● ●	● ● ●	● ● ●
Hotels, restaurants, and shops with security guards				●	●
Places where it is very dark at night and lonely	●	● ●	● ● ●	● ● ●	
Guest houses near the road				●	● ●
Places frequented by the Bong Thom (big brothers)	● ●	●	● ● ●	● ● ●	● ● ● ●
During heavy traffic hours (8 am and 5 pm)	● ●	●	● ● ●		● ● ● ●
Sweet-talking male tourists			● ● ●	●	● ●

Analysis and discussion: An analysis of the information above shows that the children had very clear indicators on the basis of which they considered each location safe or unsafe. The places considered unsafe were quite numerous, and varied in danger at different times of the day. Generally, the children were aware

....

51 If desired, an additional row can be added for the "most unsafe place." Note that several of the boxes in the example had to be left empty because the criteria did not apply.

that they should steer clear of such spots at particular times. For example, certain places were not considered safe when it was dark. They regularly adhered to these considerations when they had enough money for their survival and other needs. However, when they were desperate for money, they had to take the calculated risk of going to such places. Sadly, because of this, they often became victims of abuse or violence. Being aware of such information gives NGO staff and others opportunities to discuss safety issues, strategies for staying safe, and programming needs and desires with the children.

WHO WE ARE
....

Exercise 7:

MATRIX RANKING OF FOOD

Our Favorite Foods

Overview: The "matrix ranking of food" exercise is carried out with children to see why they prefer certain foods and their perception of the value of their preferred foods.

Description: This exercise is conducted with a focus group of children in the seven- to fifteen-year-old age group. Variations of this exercise can include working with children in different age groups, as well as "boys only" and "girls only" groups. *The purpose of the exercise is to learn about the group's perception of the value of various types of food.*

Method: To carry out this exercise, we first establish rapport with the group and then explain that we want to find out details about the food that they eat, and the advantages of each type of food. The matrix ranking is carried out in the same way as a normal matrix ranking (see exercise 5). Ask the group to name five to seven of their favorite foods. List or draw pictures of these across the top of a large sheet of paper. Down the left side of the paper, write the reasons that the children give for liking these particular food items. When this list of reasons is completed, ask the children to look over the entire chart and choose their favorite. For example, you can ask, "If among all of these, you could choose only one, which would it be?" Place a 1 by this item, and then continue to rank each type of food in the final row. As in the previous exercise, when two items are ranked equally, use an equal sign and then skip one number to keep the rankings consistent.

Expected output: The following is an example of this exercise:

Reasons for liking this food	Top Seven Favorite Food Items						
	Meat	Rice	Vegetables	Fish	Bor-Bor (porridge)	Noodles	Num Pang (bread)
Easily available at home	● ● ● ● ● ●	●	●	● ● ●	● ● ●	● ● ●	● ● ● ● ●
Cheap to buy	● ● ● ● ●	●	● ●	● ●	● ● ●	● ● ● ● ●	● ● ● ● ● ●
Tasty	●	● ● ● ● ● ●	● ● ● ●	● ● ● ●	● ●	● ● ●	● ● ●
Don't feel hungry afterwards (satisfaction)	● ● ● ●	● ● ●	● ● ●	● ● ● ●	● ●	●	● ● ●
Eaten during celebrations	●	● ● ● ● ●	● ● ● ●	● ● ●	● ● ● ● ●	● ●	● ● ●
Regularly eaten at home	● ● ● ● ●	●	● ●	● ● ●	● ● ●	● ● ●	● ● ● ●
Makes you feel strong (removes weakness)	● ● ●	● ● ●	● ● ●	● ● ● ● ●	●	● ●	● ● ● ● ●
Favorite	●	● ● ● ●	● ● ● ●	● ● ● ●	● ● ● ● ●	● ● ●	● ●

Analysis and discussion: An analysis of the output from one such exercise shows that for this group, favorite food items were usually available, had a satisfying effect, and removed hunger. Nutritional value was not an important consideration to this group. It seems that this group did not know many things about nutrition or the nutritive values of the foods they regularly ate. One potential outcome of this finding could be a training exercise for children about nutrition and the value of various foods for the human body.

Exercise 8:

MATRIX RANKING OF SCHOOL SUBJECTS

Our Favorite Subjects in School

Overview: The matrix ranking of school subjects is carried out to find out what subjects the children like best and the reasons that they like those subjects.

Description: This exercise is conducted with a group of school-going children in middle school. *The purpose of the exercise is to find out about their favorite subjects and the reasons why they like these subjects.*

Method: To carry out this exercise, invite a group of eight to ten middle-school-aged children who regularly attend middle school. After establishing good rapport with the group of boys and girls, explain the purpose of the exercise. Then, using a large sheet of paper, ask them to list the top five subjects that they like to study in school. List these across the top of the paper. Down the left side of the page, ask the students to list the various reasons for which they picked the five subjects as their favorites. After the list is complete, rank the five subjects as seen below for each of the criteria. For the final row, ask the children to choose their favorite based on all of the reasons. For example, you can ask, "If you could only choose one subject from all of these as your favorite, which would it be?" Place a 1 by this item, and then continue to rank each subject in the final row. In cases where they consider two subjects to have the same ranking use the (=) sign against both subjects that are equal in rank. Skip the next consecutive number and continue numbering the rest of the subjects (i.e., 1, 2=, 2=, 4, 5).

Expected output: The following is an example of this exercise:

Reasons for liking the subject	Top Five Favorite Subjects				
	Mathematics	**Language**	**Geography**	**Science**	**Social Studies**
Interesting	• •	•	• • • •	• • •	• • • •
Easy to understand	• •	•	• • • •	• • •	• • • • •
Easy to get good marks	•	• • • •	• • •	• •	• • • •
Learn new things	• •	• • • •	•	• •	• • • •
Useful in everyday life	•	• •	• • • •	• • •	• • • •
Fun while learning	•	• • • •	• • • •	• •	• • • •
Feel important after learning	• •	• • •	• • • •	• • • •	•
Can use at home to impress parents	•	• •	• • • •	• • • •	• •
Favorite	•	• •	• • • • •	• • •	• • • •

Analysis and discussion: An analysis of the information collected from facilitating this exercise shows the reasons why school-going students consider various subjects to be their favorites. The criteria used are those that the students themselves determined, and these are likely to change from one community to another. It is also clear that some of the reasons that the children liked various subjects were related to how they felt afterwards, having learned something. They were particularly happy with subjects that helped them feel important afterwards in being able to use their new knowledge at home to help their parents like with mathematics, or with sharing new learning at home related to what they learned in social studies. Especially in rural areas, children who go to school often understand the sacrifices that their parents make to send them to school. Children, therefore, want to make a good impression on their parents in being able to demonstrate to them the value of the education that they are receiving.

WHO WE ARE
....

Exercise 9:

IMPORTANT FEATURES OF CHILDREN'S LIVES

The Four Cards of Life

Overview: Using four cards, children can describe themselves, their families, their schools, and their communities.

Description: The "four cards of life" exercise encourages children to draw and write about their lives from four different angles: "myself," "my family," "my school," and "my community." *The purpose of this exercise is to learn from children about the important features of their lives.*

Method: This activity should only be done with small groups of children who are old enough to read and write. Beforehand, prepare the cards by cutting sheets of paper in half (about 15 x 21 cm for A4 paper or 5.5 x 8.5 in. for letter) in a variety of different colors. Start by giving each child a set of four cards. One option is to give each child four cards of the same color and use a different color for each child. Another option is to give each child four different colored cards. Either way is acceptable, as long as you clearly explain what you would like for the children to do with the cards. Ask the children to write and draw different things on each of the cards as follows:

- Card 1, *"Myself"*: Here, the children are asked to describe themselves, their situations, their feelings of self-worth, their economic status, and their educational status. If it is appropriate to the context, you can ask the children to include their spiritual beliefs on this card.
- Card 2, *"My Family"*: Using this card, each child can describe her or his family, who each person is, what the family members do, how healthy each person is, and the child's relationship with each member of the family. Ask the children to draw small pictures of their houses as well.
- Card 3, *"My School"*: Ask the children to write about the school they attend, having them include the sort of situation that exists in the school (safe or unsafe, enjoyable, difficult, etc.), the types of relationships there, the attitudes of the school authorities toward the children, and how the child feels about the school environment.
- Card 4, *"My Community"*: With this card, ask each child to describe his or her community and the type of people who live there, their attitudes and behavior toward the child, and the type of care and support that the child receives from them.

Encourage the children to write at least five to seven sentences for each card. This can be in the form of bullet points, and they can include a few small drawings if they wish.

Expected output: When the children have finished creating their cards, invite them to exchange the cards with one another so that each child has someone else's cards. Next, ask the children to take turns reading the cards in their hands out loud for the group. Begin with Card 1, "Myself" for each child, and then move through the cards in order until you reach Card 4, "My Community."

To be able to follow up any challenges or issues that arise during the discussion, have a teammate serve as the documenter for the game. The documenter can keep track of the different bits of information that emerge and the number of times they arise. Then, the information can be summarized by calculating the total number of children and the percent who mentioned each challenge or issue related to self, family, school, and community.

Analysis and discussion: After the children have had a chance the share, the facilitator should sit among them, give a quick review of some of the profiles shared, and summarize how the children in the group feel about their situations. This is an excellent starting point for further discussions about the status and treatment of individual children and all children within the community. Spiritual beliefs, self-worth, family relationships, educational opportunities, and community programs can all be evaluated using this exercise. In addition, this exercise can also help you to hear insights from the children on the way to bring changes and improvements to their lives.

To move the process one level deeper, you can have a focus group discussion with the participants, asking them for their advice on the best way to overcome a specific problem or challenge that was discussed.

Exercise 10:
SELF-ESTEEM AND SELF-WORTH ANALYSIS

What about Me?

Overview: This exercise can help us learn about how children feel about themselves.

Description: A child's perception of herself or himself is important. *The purpose of this exercise is to find out how children view themselves, and how they believe that other people view them.*

Method: This exercise can be facilitated with individual children, or with a small group. In groups, it usually works best to play with either all girls or all boys of around the same age. First, draw three columns on a large piece of paper. Fill in the left column as shown below. Next, explain how the Ten-Seed Technique (TST) works, and then ask the children to distribute ten seeds in the middle column to illustrate how they feel about themselves. In the right column, write the reasons that the children give as they explain their choices for placing seeds.

Expected output: The following is an example of this exercise, facilitated with a group of street children:

Self-Esteem and Self-Worth	# of Seeds
"I am a precious human being who is valued by others"	
"I am of some value" (only a few of my friends care for me, because we help and take care of each other)	● ● ● ● ●
"I am worthless and of no value" (no one cares for me, and those who do, do so for their own benefit)	● ● ● ● ●

Analysis and discussion: It is not surprising to see the way the seeds are distributed by this group of street children. Many of them considered themselves to be worthless. They had experienced abandonment, abuse, and rejection, and many had been used by their families for financial gain.

Bad experiences weigh heavily on children's minds. Some people would claim that this contributes to the desire to only live for the moment and to try anything that takes their fancy. If this is the case, however, it also makes the children very vulnerable to exploitation. On the other hand, many street children have very strong friendships with their peers (even when some friends steal from each other!), because they can understand and accept one another.

One of the hardest tasks for those working with street children is to improve their sense of self-esteem and self-worth. This exercise is a starting point—you can learn about how children view themselves and listen with respect to their thoughts. From this knowledge, you can start to help them build more self-esteem and self-worth by treating them with dignity, explaining how valuable they are in God's eyes,[52] and developing trusting relationships with them. It requires persistent effort and the development of a long-term relationship before children are able to overcome their skepticism and perceive that the adults truly do care for them.

....

52   For more on the dignity and inherent value of children, see McConnell, Orona, and Stockley, eds., *Understanding God's Heart for Children.*

* * *

Exercise 11:

PERSONAL EMPOWERMENT ASSESSMENT

How Strong Am I?

Overview: This exercise can help us learn about how empowered children feel.

Description: Empowerment "enables people to make choices, to have a voice and become agents of change."[53] Many organizations seek to empower children, but how effective is their work? *The purpose of this exercise is to find out how empowered or disempowered children believe themselves to be, and to give organizations insight into more effective ways to empower children.*

Method: With a group of seven- to sixteen-year-old children, briefly discuss the concept of empowerment. Be sure to use terms that they understand. For example, you could ask questions about what choices children can make by themselves, or what things in the community children feel like they can change without help from adults.

Once you are sure that the children understand the concept of empowerment, show them a large chart with the left column filled in as shown in the example below. Ask the children to divide up ten seeds in the middle column, and record their explanations in the right column.

....
53   Graham Gordon, *Understanding Advocacy* (Teddington, UK: Tearfund, 2002), 20, http://tilz. tearfund.org/webdocs/Tilz/Roots/English/Advocacy%20toolkit/Advocacy%20toolkit_E_FULL%20 DOC_Parts%20A%2BB.pdf.

Expected output: The following is an example of this exercise, facilitated with a group of street children:

Level of Empowerment	# of Seeds	Remarks
Fully empowered (I am able to interact with others in society to bring changes into my own life)		Not able to independently negotiate
Partially empowered (I am able to negotiate some changes because of a law, the work of an NGO, etc.)	● ● ● ● ● ●	With assistance, able to make some changes because of the work of the NGO
Disempowered (I am completely at the mercy of others)	● ● ● ●	Helpless to change how we are treated by authorities Some situations even out of the control of NGOs

Analysis and discussion: When this exercise took place, the children rightly pointed out that they did not feel very empowered. When they were not with a group, they often felt helpless in situations where they come face to face with authorities who made decisions that would impact them. For instance, the police would regularly clear them out of a particular place or prevent them from entering an area where they would come to earn income. Even when assisted and supported by NGOs, they were conscious that the level of empowerment that they had was only based on continued support from the NGO, and the type of empowerment that they had was only to be "assigned and informed."[54] They had not had any major contribution into the process by way of their own initiative or their own ideas.

The children had also seen that the NGO was helpless in certain situations with the authorities. Empowerment is closely related to many other things like self-worth, protection, and feelings of security and peacefulness. Hence, in some cases, this exercise can help organizations to understand more fully how their own level of empowerment (or disempowerment) can affect the children. Organizations can also use this exercise to learn how they can be more effective in empowering children.

....

54 Hart, *Children's Participation*. See also http://www.freechild.org/ladder.htm.

* * *

Exercise 12:

ENTERTAINMENT AND
INNOVATION PROFILE

The Games We Play

Overview: This exercise is designed to find out about the games that children play on their own.

Description: Designed to explore with the children the games that they play when they are on their own, this exercise is used to determine the popularity of each games and how the children determine the rules for the game and who the winner is. *The purpose of the exercise is to find out how children keep themselves entertained and find out how they innovate in designing games.*

Method: This exercise is done with a large group of children and is usually preceded by one or two games that involve all the children present. Facilitators also join in the game to help build relationships. After playing the games, ask everyone to sit down around a large sheet of paper. Have the children list the names of the various games they play. Along with the name of the game, ask them to draw a picture representing the game (see below). Next, ask them to vote for the most popular game using seeds. Give each child three or four seeds, depending on the total number of games listed (i.e., use more seeds if there is a long list of games). Have the children place one seed each on the pictures representing their favorite games.

Expected output: The following diagram shows the output generated from such an exercise:

Analysis and discussion: This exercise usually results in quite a lot of chaos as the children often become very excited to vote for their favorite games. It

is necessary to be on hand and allow for small variations, where some children may want to vote using fewer seeds and some may wish for more seeds. Take care not to give too many seeds as the exercise is intended to encourage the children to a few favorite games, and if different children receive different numbers of seeds, the results may not really reflect the preferences of the entire group. The names of the games, as given by the children themselves, are very interesting, since they show how innovative and creative children can be. Finding the total number of seeds placed for each game shows which game is the most popular.

Ideally, game-listing exercise should be followed by another exercise in which the group creates an inventory of games played by children. This is done by listing the games and collecting further details on each of them. The creation of this inventory should be considered a work in progress, with more details added on as they become available. Many games are seasonal, hence details are likely to be remembered only later when the season to play that particular game arrives.

It is interesting particularly to see how the rules for the same game vary from village to village. Often, these rules are only partly known to the chil-

dren, and they create more rules as they go. It is interesting to see how, sometimes, the game comes to a standstill because of a dispute about the rules. On such an occasion, there is often a heated dispute, and the rule is modified or a new one introduced to enable the game to continue. These decisions are almost always by consensus. Observing these types of activities, discussions, and decisions can help us to understand how children view the world and how

they interact in relationships. When observed carefully, the games children play can demonstrate their resourcefulness, innovation, and creativity.

#	Name of Game (local name)	Materials Required	Brief Description of Game and Rules	Season When It is Played	Remarks
1					
2					
3					
4					
5					
6					
7					

* * *

OUR ACTIVITIES

....

Exercise 13:
ACTIVITY PROFILE

A Normal Day in Our Lives

Overview: This exercise is conducted to find out how children in a community spend their days.

Description: Daily activities are very important in the lives of children, and they vary significantly from child to child within a community. *The purpose of this exercise is to explore and compare the profiles of an average day in the lives of various children in the community, especially those who do not go to school. This exercise can also be used to compare gender differences.*[55]

Method: After an initial discussion with the entire group, divide the children into two groups, one for children who attend school and one for children who do not attend school. Then, divide each of these groups into two smaller groups of boys and girls. This will give you four groups of children:

1. Boys attending school
2. Boys not attending school
3. Girls attending school
4. Girls not attending school

....

55   For more on gender differences see exercises 4 and 11.

For each group, make a chart with four columns. In the left column, mark the hours of the day. Ask the children to write down various activities they are busy with throughout the day in the second column, labeled "activities."

Have them try to explain what they would normally be doing for the entire twenty-four-hour period. After the groups fill in their activities on the charts, give each group twenty-four seeds and ask them to distribute these according to the length of time they spend in each activity. If the twenty-four seeds are confusing for the children, you can have them use ten seeds instead. The seeds will fill in the third column of the chart.[56] Finally, fill in the fourth column with any special remarks or notes that the children make about the activities. For example, they may note that their daily routines vary on certain days of the week.

Have each of the small groups share their charts with the larger group, then facilitate a discussion about the differences between the groups' activities throughout the day.

Expected output: The following diagram shows the output generated from such an exercise conducted with school-going male children:

Time	Activities	Number of Seeds	Remarks
00:00	Go to sleep	• • •	
01:00		• • •	
02:00			
03:00			
04:00			
05:00			

. . . .

56 Another option is to do this exercise with selected individuals instead of groups of children. As noted above, the exercise can be done with either twenty-four or ten seeds.

06:00	Wash up and do household chores	•	
07:00	Complete chores, eat and leave for school	•	
08:00	Attend school	• • • •	
09:00			
10:00			
11:00			
12:00	Home for lunch, rest, then back to school and play until class starts	• •	
13:00			
14:00	In school	• • •	
15:00			
16:00			
17:00	Return home, play	•	
18:00	Help at home and study (do school homework)	•	
19:00	Dinner, television	•	
20:00	Go to sleep	• •	
21:00		• •	
22:00			
23:00			

Analysis and discussion: To analyze the information, compare the charts from each of the four groups. It is clear that this group of boys has a fairly well spaced life with enough time to play and rest and only minor responsibilities for helping at home. However, when this chart is compared to the average day of a girl from this community, the sharp contrast is immediately visible. Girls have far less time for sleep. They spend much more time helping with the household chores, and they have less time to play. Information like this will make it clear why there is thus a natural predisposition for girls to drop out of school in greater numbers than boys. Again, when we compare this with the lot of a child domestic worker (increasingly known as CDW in development circles), the picture is very dismal. On a particular occasion, we used the Ten-Seed Technique (TST) to find out what the average day of a CDW was like. When we placed the ten seeds in front of her to group and show how she spent her time, she replied, "Ten seeds are too few to show that!" When we persisted, she started grouping the seeds and the following was the profile she showed us of her average day:

Average Day in the Life of a Child Domestic Worker	
Washing all clothes of the employer's family and ironing clothes	● ● ●
Cleaning the house (sweeping, mopping) and other preparations in the house	● ● ●
Cooking for the whole household	● ●
Take care of the children of the employer	● ●

When the exercise is finished, the information should be shared with the adults who make decisions in the community. Information from the various groups can encourage the decision makers to find ways to negotiate and obtain more time for the affected children to spend on study or developing future life skills. This can be done and has been done, even for the most oppressed CDWs, as demonstrated by several non-governmental organizations in Cambodia working with vulnerable children.

OUR ACTIVITIES
....

Exercise 14:
SEASONAL ACTIVITIES

What We Do Throughout the Year

Overview: The seasonal analysis exercise is facilitated with the children's focus group to find out the types of activities that they are involved in over the course of a year.

Description: This exercise can be conducted with a group of children to understand the types of activities that regularly occur each year and change with the various seasons. *The purpose of this exercise is to write down the types of activities that occur, understand the children's perspectives about these, and identify times that are either overloaded or relatively free so that external interventions, when required, can take these busy and relatively free times into account.*

Method: To carry out this exercise, identify a group of representative seven- to fifteen-year-old boys and girls from the community. After briefing and building rapport with this group, provide them with twelve large stones or bricks and ask them to lay these out in a row representing the twelve months of a calendar year. After this is done, ask the group to list the various activities that they are involved with as children. A list of this is prepared (as shown in the diagram) with drawings or diagrams where possible. After the list is prepared, provide the group with ten seeds for each of the activities so that they can distribute these over the twelve months of the year to show the intensity of the activity at different times of the year. Use different colored seeds for each of the activities, and keep asking questions to ensure you understand the logic behind the distribution of the seeds. Try to manage with ten seeds for each of the issues, and only give additional seeds in the rarest of situations (as in the last two rows of the diagram below).

Expected output: The following example shows how the output from carrying out such an exercise might look:

Activity	Jan	Feb	Mar	Apr	May	Jun
Rainfall						• •
Agriculture				•	•	• •
Cold Weather	• • •					
School	•	•	•	•		• •
Holidays (Vacations)					• • • • • • •	
Sickness	• •			•		• •
Fun Times	•	• •				
Difficult Times					• • • •	
Playing Games	•	•	•	•	•	•
Helping in the House	•	•	•	•	•	•

Activity	Jul	Aug	Sep	Oct	Nov	Dec
Rainfall	• • •	• • •	• •			
Agriculture			• •	• •		• •
Cold Weather					• •	• • • • •
School	•	•			•	•
Holidays (Vacations)						• • • •
Sickness	• •					• • •
Fun Times				• • •	• • •	•
Difficult Times			• •	• •		• •
Playing Games	•	•	•	•	•	•
Helping in the House	•	•	•	•	•	•

Analysis and discussion: An analysis of the exercise on the seasonal activities among children shows that children were involved in a wide range of activities over the course of a year. For the last two categories, they required more seeds to show that the activities occurred with equal importance throughout the year. Even in seasons of heavy rain, when going out was very difficult, they were always able to have fun and find some game to play. While the children were often affected by minor ailments throughout the year, their identification of December, January, and February as particular seasons of illness was related to times when they were sick and laid up in bed, unable to go outside. Interestingly, the fun times were those times in the post-harvest season when they had plenty at home, and also when they had plenty of time to play. The difficult times were those when they had vacations from school, but when there was increasing interference from grown-ups in their activities.

* * *

OUR ACTIVITIES
....

Exercise 15:
IMPORTANT EVENTS IN CHILDREN'S LIVES

The River of Life

Overview: The "river of life" exercise encourages children to explain the events that they believe are important in the past, present, and future of their lives.

Description: This exercise consists of working with a small group of children and asking them to draw their lives in a drawing like a river.[57] *The purpose of this exercise is to find out directly from the children about the events that they consider important in their lives.*

Method: With individual children or small groups of children who are old enough to draw, explain that you would like for them to draw a river that stands for their lives. Each child is to use images like rocks, curves in the river, and so on to show the beginning of her or his life and significant things that have happened since then. The depiction should lead up to the present state of his or her life, and in some cases, the children may also want to depict the future. After the children finish their drawings, ask each one to describe their river of life either in the group or on a one-to-one basis with the facilitator.

....

57   If the children in your area are not familiar with rivers, you may wish to adjust the exercise. For example, you could ask the children to draw a "path of life" instead.

This exercise often works very well with children who live close to rivers, especially when their lives are intricately connected to the river with regards to food, income, or safety.

Expected output: At the end of this exercise, each child should have a drawing of a river, and each child should have had a chance to share their drawing either with the group or individually with the facilitator.

Analysis and discussion: Instead of adults assuming what the important events are in children's lives, this exercise gives us a way to ask children to show us what they believe are the important things that have happened in their lives.

Recently, Dr. Dusadee Charoensuk of Kasetsart University in Bangkok, Thailand described the results of conducting such an exercise with children orphaned by HIV and AIDS. Two stories stood out as powerful and moving descriptions of how children understand their lives.

One boy drew his life as a boat on a river, and the river was so wide that he could not see the shores. Another young girl drew a river with three fish in it, two big and one small. She then pointed out that it was her family of three, and that now the two big fish (her parents) were dead, and she was all alone.[58]

Participating in the "river of life" exercise allowed these children a chance to express their thoughts and feelings about their circumstances, and provided the adults with a clearer understanding of what types of assistance could be most helpful to the children.

....

58   Dusadee Charoensuk, "Needs, Self-esteem and Health Impact Assessment of Orphans Due to AIDS in Thailand" (presentation at the international conference, "Sustainable Development for Peace: New Dimensions of Friendly Cooperation in the Upper Mekong Sub-region," Phnom Penh, Kingdom of Cambodia, September 25–28, 2006).

* * *

OUR ACTIVITIES

Exercise 16:
Create Your Own Exercise!

Title:

Overview (What does this exercise teach us?):

Description (What is the exercise like? What is its purpose?):

Method (How will the exercise be facilitated?):

(Draw a diagram or paste a photo here.)

Expected output:

_____

_____

_____

_____

(Show what the results will look like here.)

_____

_____

_____

_____

Analysis and discussion (What can be learned from this exercise?):

_____

_____

_____

_____

PROBLEM SOLVING
....

Exercise 17:
PROBLEM ANALYSIS
Things That Make Us Sad

Problem Analysis A: What We Are Unhappy About

Overview: The problem analysis exercise is done to find out the kind of problems that children in a community face. This exercise can be done by itself or as a part of the Holistic Worldview Analysis.[59]

Description: This exercise is conducted in order to gain an understanding of the types of problems that children face in a particular community. *The purpose of the exercise is to understand the children's perspectives of the problems that they face.*

Method: Often, children find it difficult to describe their problems. To assist them in identifying and describing their problems, help them to talk about the things that they do not like, or things that make them unhappy. Once the group of seven- to fifteen-year-old children understands, use the Ten-Seed Technique (TST) to explore their world and find out what causes them to feel unhappy. This is done in two parts: 1) What we are unhappy about, and 2) What we don't like.

....
59   See section 3, lesson 5.

Expected output: The following diagram shows the output generated from an exercise conducted to find out what makes children unhappy:

What They Are Unhappy About	
They don't get to sleep well at night	● ●
Being beaten and scolded by parents	● ●
When parents don't buy them the things they want	● ● ●
Getting poor results in school	● ● ●

Analysis and discussion: In this particular community, it was interesting to see what the children were unhappy about. While three of the situations were related to their homes and families (inadequate sleep, scolding and punishment

from parents, parents not buying them the things they wanted), the fourth thing that made them unhappy was when they obtained poor results in school and felt like they had disappointed their parents. While these issues will change from place to place and community to community, it is interesting to see that the issues that they discuss are often related to the children's individuality and desire to be treated with respect.

Problem Analysis B: What We Don't Like

Expected output: The following diagram shows the output generated from the second part of the exercise, where we try to find out what the children do not like:

What They Don't Like					
Don't like fighting and shouting	●	●	●	●	●	●
Cutting trees and plucking flowers	●	●				
Grazing cows	●					
Wandering about	●					

Analysis and discussion: In this community, the things that the children did not like were related to strained relationships, which resulted in fighting and shouting. They also disliked the cutting of trees, indiscriminate plucking of flowers, wasting time wandering around, and being given the task of supervising the cattle. The use of the terms "unhappy" and "don't like" helped to draw out issues in the community that impacted the children from several different angles. Using the diagram that results from this exercise, can enable extended discussion on each of the things that they don't like to find out how it actually affects them. Their council on ways to improve the situation can also be sought and then discussed with those in the village who have the capacity to make changes.

PROBLEM SOLVING
....

Exercise 18:
BLESSING ANALYSIS

Things That Make Us Happy

Overview: This exercise examines the activities that children enjoy. It can be done by itself or as a part of the Holistic Worldview Analysis.[60]

Description: Children have strengths, hopes, and desires. They know what they like, and when they are encouraged to share their likes and dislikes, the community can develop a clearer picture of how the children view things. *The purpose of the exercise is to draw information about what makes children happy, and to get details for the worldview analysis to be conducted later.*

Method: Invite a focus group of children of ages seven to fifteen to join in this exercise, and spend time building rapport with them. Often, it is quite easy to obtain an initial list of enjoyable activities from the children, but it is more difficult and time-consuming to develop consensus about the placement of the seeds. Give the children ten seeds, and ask them to group the seeds together to represent the things that make them happy. To make this clearer, sometimes it may be necessary to ask them what they like.

Expected output: The following diagram shows the output generated from such an exercise:

....
60   See section 3, lesson 5.

What Makes Them Happy	
Going to school	● ● ● ● ●
Doing housework	● ● ●
Playing	● ●
Planting flowers	●

Analysis and discussion: We often presume about children that they only like to play all the time, and this is what will make them happy. Interestingly enough, in this community, the thing that made children happiest was going to school, followed by helping with the chores at home, playing, and planting flowers. This will vary from community to community, especially where the schoolteachers are not good, or never turn up. Household chores, when they take a long time or become oppressive to the point of almost becoming like child labor will also not be too attractive to children. As with all the exercises, taking the information from these exercises and presenting it to the rest of the larger group of children is very important to find out if the small group's views are the same as the larger group's views. This whole process is called *triangulation* and is essential to ensure that the opinions are representative of the whole child community.

At this feedback session, it is possible also to involve some of the smaller children whom it is difficult to keep the attention of during normal focus group discussions. Drawings and diagrams can also help the younger children to understand. The feedback sessions must also be facilitated by someone who knows how to interact with and keep the interest of small children. When the children disagree with something or ask for it to be modified, this must be immediately done in their presence.

In the picture above, taken during one such feedback session, one can see the great interest with which children are observing the presentations.

PROBLEM SOLVING

. . . .

Exercise 19:
UNCERTAINTY ANALYSIS

Things We Are Unsure About

Overview: The uncertainty analysis exercise is conducted with a group of children to find out about the uncertainties that they face as a group.

Description: This exercise is designed to find out the types of uncertainties that children face. *The purpose of this exercise is to find out what the children perceive as the uncertainties in their lives, and to provide information for the Holistic Worldview Analysis.*[61]

Method: The focus group for this exercise also consists of children aged seven to fifteen. After opening with rapport-building exercises, ask the group questions about the things that make them uncertain, things that seem to change without warning, and things that children are unsure about. When the group has agreed on the main categories, ask them to use the Ten-Seed Technique (TST) to identify how uncertain they feel about each category.

Expected output: The following diagram shows the output generated from such an exercise:

. . . .
61   See section 3, lesson 5.

Uncertainty Analysis					
Parents stop children from playing without warning	●	●	●	●	●
Sudden additional chores during school holidays		●	●	●	
Illness		●			
Crop failure or low harvest		●			

Analysis and discussion: It is interesting to study the information provided by the focus group of children, and particularly to notice the sharp contrast between the results from the group of adults and the group of children. Here, a major part of the uncertainties that children experienced were related to their playtime. As our discussions with the children developed, they grew more animated about these issues. The children were able to voice with genuine feeling their strong opinions.

One thing that they felt strongly about was the way their parents sometimes suddenly interrupted their games. Even when the children were intensely involved in a game, the parents would ask them to stop immediately and return home. One young boy was very emotional about this, and exclaimed, "How can they just stop the game just like that? Especially when I was winning!" There were tears in his eyes and his face was flushed red with anger as he spoke.

Another unknown for the children occurred during school vacations, when the children did not have fixed times to play. This caused considerable stress to the children, for they never knew when their games would be interrupted, or when parents would come to the group, ask them to break up their game immediately, and return home to do some additional work.

Of course, things that affect adults, like illness and poor harvests, also affect children. These make less food available at home and lengthen the time of struggle during food shortages. Children in this community mentioned that on such occasions, they tried to stay out of sight without making too much noise as they played. Adults sitting around in small groups talking in hushed tones were their indicators of such times of difficulty, when erring children were most likely to get severely punished. Most of the children could recall such times in the recent past when they had to "strategically lay low." All the children knew of hideouts away in the village where they went at such times. During times of plenty and happy times for the grownups, children were more welcome to run about and scream and play without any interference from the grownups.

Such exercises also provide an excellent opportunity to talk to the adults in the community, helping them to become more sensitive to their children's needs.

PROBLEM SOLVING
....

Exercise 20:
INDEPENDENCE ASSESSMENT

What Can I Do By Myself?

Overview: This exercise seeks to find out how dependent or independent children are in a number of different areas of life.

Description: Using several large pieces of paper and the Ten-Seed Technique (TST), this exercise assesses what sorts of things children can do by themselves and what sorts of things they cannot do by themselves. *The purpose of this exercise is to assess the child's perspective on her or his level of independence in four main areas: the physical dimension, the psychological dimension, the social dimension, and the environmental dimension.*

Method: This exercise works best with a group of older children (ten to sixteen years) who are close to the same age. Before meeting with the children, prepare four large sheets of paper by drawing three columns and filling in the left column for each, as shown below. After building rapport with the group, show them the first chart, "Physical Dimension," and ask them to use the TST to place seeds in the middle column. Note their responses and comments in the right column. Continue this process with ten more seeds each for the "Psychological Dimension" chart, the "Social Dimension" chart, and the "Environmental Dimension" chart.

The physical dimension can be described as our ability to live, earn, and work independently.

Expected output: The examples below show the responses of one group of children living on the street:

I) Physical Dimension	# of Seeds	Remarks
Totally dependent on others		
Partially dependent on others	● ● ●	Protection needs Healthcare needs Charity support during difficult times
Completely independent	● ● ● ● ● ● ●	Most times we can earn sufficient money to take care of our needs Have made our own community structures to take care of our needs

Analysis and discussion: Street children are usually quite independent and know how to survive on the streets. Therefore, they consider themselves physically independent, and they know that they can create their own small community of street children. I have often seen street children moving about as small groups or families. However, they do need the support of adults when they are sick or in trouble, or when they are vulnerable to attacks or exploitation. Also, they need adult support during times of crisis when they are unable to earn enough money to provide for their daily needs. From the physical perspective, therefore, this group of children sees their quality of life as being quite alright, though this is not what they say when they are trying to beg for money!

The psychological dimension includes our perception of ability to be happy and in control of one's emotions, self-image, confidence and ability to cope with sadness and worries about living.

Expected output:

2) Psychological Dimension	# of Seeds	Remarks
Totally dependent on others		
Partially dependent on others	●	Only need support very rarely for their psychological needs
Completely independent	● ● ● ● ● ● ● ● ●	Have their own circle of friends to meet these needs Manage by taking drugs when life gets tough

Analysis and discussion: Street children soon develop a philosophy of life that learns to create and develop its own survival strategies. These include a very close network of friends who stick together and form a support system that is often much stronger than conventional families. In times of difficulty, they resort to the use of drugs like sniffing glue, smoking marijuana, or taking amphetamine tablets. They describe this in Cambodia as becoming *khlang* (strong) to cope with difficult times. It is only in extremely difficult situations when they have been severely abused or beaten up that they willingly seek external support from adults. Street children usually treat the world of adults with great caution and skepticism, and they often rely much more strongly on their peers than on adults for psychological support.

The psychological dimension includes our perception of ability to relate to others, get help from others, and give support to others.

Expected output:

3) Social Dimension	# of Seeds	Remarks
Totally dependent on others		
Interdependent with other peers	● ● ● ● ●	Very close ties with other street children Strong family-like bonds with each other
Completely independent	● ● ● ● ●	Very independent financially, but very interdependent socially

Analysis and discussion: The street children's perception of their social dimension is often quite interesting as it shows that they have very strong feelings of bonding with each other. In some countries, children will travel great distances by themselves in order to visit friends in the places where they first lived on the streets.[62] Since these children (especially the ones that live and work on the streets) depend on the barest minimum infrastructure of shelter, their social network often ends up becoming that fabric that intertwines their lives to each other.

....
62   This dimension has not been studied very much; there may be a lot to learn through research about the unique features of social bonds among street children.

The psychological dimension includes our perception of their surroundings and opportunities for developing skills and getting information.

Expected output:

4) Environmental Dimension	# of Seeds	Remarks
Totally dependent on others		
Partially dependent on others	● ●	Have limited access to opportunities for improving skills and finding new information
Completely independent	● ● ● ● ● ● ● ●	Mostly have the ability to get necessary skills and information related to better opportunities

Analysis and discussion: As can be seen in the output above, some children feel that they have the ability to develop skills and find new information, while others feel that their ability is limited. The dependence (or interdependence) of street children on their peers has its own limitations, as the peers also compete for the same resources, and hence, the sharing of information and skills is always done with caution so as not to lose their own opportunities. For all of these children, NGOs and other organizations can help by providing the children with more opportunities to improve their skills and obtain information that is relevant to them.[63]

....
63 For more examples of finding new information, see exercises 23–26.

PROBLEM SOLVING
....

Exercise 21:
CAUSAL DIAGRAM OF DISEASE

What Makes Us Sick?

Overview: The causal diagram exercise is conducted to establish the connections between various causes and link these to specific diseases or illnesses that occur in a community.

Description: This exercise can be conducted in a very visual way involving the children to take part in the process so that it is also a fun activity. *The purpose of the exercise is to establish links between causes and results such as illnesses and diseases.*

Method: There are two methods for carrying out this exercise. One way is to use a large sheet of paper and write down the name of the disease in the center of the sheet and then have arrows radiate out from this, linking the disease to a variety of causes. Each cause is then further pursued to find out what causes it, and so on, until a fairly intricate diagram emerges. This is then discussed with the group to understand their perspective of the causes of disease in that particular community.

The second way of conducting the exercise is to make it a very visual and fun activity. To do this, first identify a disease, and then choose a child to represent this particular disease or illness. The rest of the children are then asked to list the causes of the disease and a child is chosen to represent each of the causes. These children are then asked to place one hand each on the person representing the disease or illness. Each child representing a cause is then linked with other sub-causes and so on, until a fairly complicated pattern of network of hands and children emerges. This is then copied onto a piece of paper.

The emerging pattern can also be used for discussing solutions and making clear links in the children's minds. The exercise can also be used to clarify the perceptions of children regarding various conditions. For example, when talking with a group of street children, it was interesting to find out what they understood about HIV and AIDS. Most of them were able to understand that it spread through four ways: through having unprotected sexual relation-

ships, through sharing needles, from mother to child, and through blood. This was obviously due to the massive effort in ensuring that this information was made available to all the children. However, when exploring further it became clear that the next related causes were not really clear. When asked how it spread through blood, there was confusion all around. Some children had this to state. "When we are walking around, and if we step on a piece of glass or some sharp object, there will be bleeding. This blood is dangerous and can give us AIDS, so we should run away from it as soon as possible!" It was obvious that while part of the information they had obtained was correct, they had drawn their own conclusions about the background and specific reasons for each cause, and this resulted in confusion and faulty beliefs.

Expected output: The following is an example of this exercise:

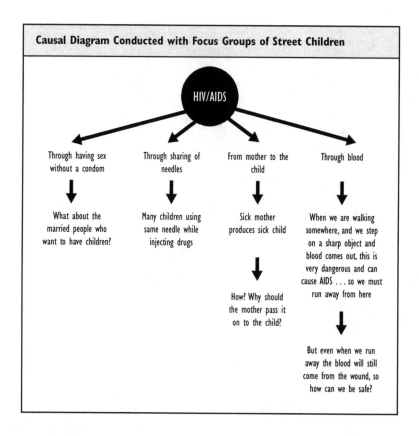

Causal Diagram Conducted with Focus Groups of Street Children

HIV/AIDS

| Through having sex without a condom | Through sharing of needles | From mother to the child | Through blood |

| What about the married people who want to have children? | Many children using same needle while injecting drugs | Sick mother produces sick child | When we are walking somewhere, and we step on a sharp object and blood comes out, this is very dangerous and can cause AIDS . . . so we must run away from here |

How? Why should the mother pass it on to the child?

But even when we run away the blood will still come from the wound, so how can we be safe?

Analysis and discussion: Analyzing the diagram shows us what the children perceive as being the cause of the disease or illness. As in the example above, children may have quite a bit of confusion related to the causes of diseases and how they spread. The children were, however, very clear about the needle sharing component. For the other three causes, the diagram itself can help become the way for the confusion to be cleared, and this can be done fairly easily. The causal diagram can also be used for studying links to other issues such as trafficking, domestic violence, school dropouts, and so on.

PROBLEM SOLVING
....

Exercise 22:
RAPID HOLISTIC
HEALTH ASSESSMENT

How Healthy Am I?

Overview: This exercise seeks to find out how healthy children are from a holistic perspective.

Description: By looking at the physical, psychological, social, and spiritual health of a child or group of children, *this exercise seeks to find out about children's perceptions of their level of health, and to learn about how NGOs and other organizations can help children to become healthier.*

Method: This exercise can be facilitated with individual children or with small groups of children (five children maximum). Beforehand, prepare four large sheets of paper by drawing three columns and filling in the left column for each, as shown below.

Invite the child or children to place ten seeds in the middle column of the first sheet to illustrate how often they get sick. Note their comments and explanations in the right column. Continue by filling in the "mind," "social," and "spiritual" charts.

Expected output: The resulting chart from such an exercise would look something like this:

1) Healthy Condition of the Body	# of Seeds	Remarks
Not good (get sick often)	• • • •	We get sick often with respiratory and digestive ailments This affects our ability to earn money
Average (get sick sometimes)	• • •	Sometimes we feel weak and exhausted
Excellent (rarely get sick)	• • •	Sometimes we have excellent health

Analysis and discussion: Physical health is very important to children, especially children living in difficult circumstances. Often, they do not make any special efforts to improve their health, but they nevertheless recognize that bad health makes life very inconvenient for them. For example, when they are sick, they often have a strong desire to rest, but since they constantly need to work in order to earn money, they must continue to work despite their discomfort and exhaustion. During times of good physical health, many children feel that illness is not very important, and they are therefore not interested in listening to any advice on best practices and the like.

Expected output:

2) Healthy Condition of the Mind	# of Seeds	Remarks
Not good (feeling agitated and upset)	• •	At times of illness, feel very depressed Discouraged
Average (not feeling peaceful and calm)	• • • • •	Feel sad and lonely, but make up for it by taking drugs
Excellent (feeling peaceful and calm)	• • •	When on top of issues and have very good earnings, feel that everything is alright

Analysis and discussion: Most local languages will have specific terms for mental peace and calm. In the Khmer language, this word is *sabai*. Make sure that you are familiar with the local term, what it means, and how it is used in order to understand the cultural pieces of the children's explanations.

For the chart about psychological health, you will notice that often, the responses will vary according to the circumstances of the child, and how long they have been experiencing difficult circumstances. Many children begin to cope better as time passes, so things that upset or agitated them before soon shift to the second level of being average. Children who live very turbulent lives must let their coping mechanisms[64] kick in very quickly. Often, when children who are used to living in difficult circumstances consider their mental health to be excellent, it may be a way of saying that they are coping well, even though the situation around them is neither positive nor healthy.

Expected output:

3) Healthy Condition of Social Relationships	# of Seeds	Remarks
Not good (relationships broken)	● ● ●	There are often clashes with others competing for the same resources Sometimes, it is best to stay out of the way of some people
Average (relationships strained)	● ● ● ● ●	A process of give and take and adjustment Have to learn how to deal with some people
Excellent (excellent relationships)	● ●	This is true only for our own small clique of friends

Analysis and discussion: Relationships are very important to children, and children will go to great lengths to maintain relationships with friends, and also to stay out of the way of those with whom they do not get along or have strained relationships. It is interesting to see how they accept a great

....

64   A "coping mechanism" is a skill that people use to reduce stress. It may be a healthy way to deal with difficult situations (like talking to a close friend) or an unhealthy way (like starting a fistfight).

deal of negative treatment from their close friends (including being cheated and having things stolen). Often, this occurs because relationships are more precious to them than possessions. Organizations that seek to work with street children must remember this important fact and ensure that they work hard to establish relationships with the children that can ultimately become transformational. Interestingly enough, instead of working toward transformation, many programs with children tend to concentrate most of their efforts on the physical resources and infrastructure that they presume the children are most deprived of.

Expected output:

4) Spiritual Health	# of Seeds	Remarks
Not interested (do not care about this aspect)	● ● ● ● ●	Not interested, but will pretend to be in order to get some benefit Every action is related to survival
Average (at times of crisis look for a higher being)	● ● ● ●	Will pray in times of crisis and extreme difficulty
Excellent (spiritually conscious)	●	Conscious of the need to have spiritual qualities like love, joy, peace, patience, kindness, goodness, faithfulness, gentleness and self-control

Analysis and discussion: An important thing to remember is that when we talk about the spiritual health of children, the natural assumption is to equate this with their religious affiliations. In this exercise, however, we are actually talking about the spiritual dimension as it relates to consciousness and awareness of the need for qualities like love, joy, peace, patience, kindness, goodness, faithfulness, gentleness, and self-control. When asked, many children will be able to think of friends who are conscious in this dimension. The succeeding discussion can then focus on the influences in the lives of these children that enabled this to happen, and how the same type of consciousness can be fostered in their lives, too. The spiritual dimension can bring about a deep healing process that can help to change some deep-seated negative attitudes the children have developed as a consequence of living and surviving in their difficult circumstances.

FINDING NEW INFORMATION

....

Exercise 23:
SOURCES OF NEW INFORMATION

How Do We Find Out about New Things?

Overview: This exercise is facilitated to find out how children obtain new information on various issues.

Description: Designed to find and discuss the various sources from which children get information on various subjects, *this exercise's purpose is to determine how children get new information on various issues, and determine how these existing sources are supplemented to ensure complete understanding on some critical issues such as disease.*

Method: This exercise is carried out using the Ten-Seed Technique (TST). After you have established rapport with the focus group of seven- to sixteen-year-old children, ask them to share about the various sources from which they get new information on various issues. After the group has brainstormed six to ten possible sources of information (such as parents, teachers, television, and so on), ask them to imagine that ten seeds represent all the sources from which they get new information. Have the children group the seeds into clusters to represent these different sources by using more seeds to represent the sources that are

used more often and fewer seeds to represent the sources that are used less often. Facilitate discussions with the small group and the larger group of children from the community to make sure that the results represent the experiences of almost all children in that community.

Expected output: The following diagram shows the output generated from such an exercise:

HIV/AIDS-related Information Sources						
PPAE.PS/CRT.01					'CHI KRENG' DISTRICT IN SIEM REAP PROVINCE	
Teachers	Friends	TV Spots	TV serials (*Taste of Life*)	Books	Community	Health Center
● ● ●			● ● ● ●	●	●	●

pilot assessment   Ravi Jayakaran/strengthening Cambodia's response to HIV/AIDS/MoEYS-DFID-UNDP partnership

Analysis and discussion: The exercise above was used for collecting information about the ways in which school-going children obtained information about HIV and AIDS. The analysis showed that approximately 25 percent of the information obtained was through their teachers, 5 percent through friends, 5 percent through television spots, 35 percent through a television series (called *Taste of Life*), 15 percent through reading books, 5 percent through the community in which they lived, and 10 percent through the health center in their village. In addition, a further analysis can be carried out to see which source of information is the clearest and most efficient. This is done by checking each source and dividing the seeds for each category into two subgroups—"clear" or "not so clear."

Based on the information that you learn from this exercise, you can identify and build on the efficient method for communication. For instance, for the primary school children in the group described above, television was the most authoritative source for new information, followed by teachers and then books. Younger children were less likely to believe information given by their peers or the community in which they lived. On the other hand, for children in secondary school, the most efficient way to pass on information on HIV and AIDS was through their peers. This key difference between the age groups may vary in different contexts, but it is an important issue to consider when trying to share information about health, safety, and more with children.

* * *

Exercise 24:
SIGNIFICANT ADULTS

Which Adults Do We Know, and How Do They Help Us?

Overview: This game is played to find out from the children who the significant adults in their lives are, and what types of roles those adults play.

Description: While adults can often provide new information for children, many of the children that we work with have learned not to trust adults. It is important to know which adults the children feel they can trust, and who they go to in order to get help. *The purpose of this exercise is to find out which adults the children feel that they know, and how those adults help the children.*

Method: This exercise can be facilitated with individual children or groups of children who are close to the same age. Usually, the exercise works best with children between the ages of seven and sixteen. When selecting individuals to participate in this exercise, look for children who might be representative or typical of the group so that their answers will most closely reflect the attitudes of the entire group.

To facilitate the exercise, first divide a large sheet of paper in three columns. Next, ask the children who the important adults in their lives are, listing their answers down the left column of the paper. Give the children ten seeds and ask them to decide how many seeds should be placed in each box of the middle column. As they discuss how to place the seeds, note their comments and remarks in the right column.

Expected output: The following is an output generated from facilitating this exercise with a group of street children:[65]

Significant Adult in Your Life	# of Seeds	Remarks
Parent(s)	●	Mostly one or other original single parent, some with stepparents
Relative	● ● ●	Usually a distant relative
Caretaker	●	An acquaintance from the same village, often someone who is benefiting from them economically
Bong Thom	● ●	Literally means "big brother," but is often the term used to refer to the local gang leaders
NGO staff	● ● ●	The NGO staff are still in the process of becoming a growing influence

Analysis and discussion: The example above shows the types of adults that had an influence in the lives of the street children. Even those that lived entirely on their own had to seek out and find some type of interface with adults in order to survive. In some cases, the adults were the *Bong Thom*, or the grown-up street children who had now become local gang leaders.

Later, this exercise can be taken to the next level by asking the same group of children about the type of influence that each of the adults has in their lives. Is it financial? Does it relate to safety? This information can help those who seek

....

65   It is important to remember that though many of the examples here are given in relation to use of the games and exercises with street children, they can work equally well also with other groups of children.

to help the children to understand how they perceive their needs, what types of adults they trust, and how they interact with the significant adults in their lives.

Exercise 25:
FINDING INFORMATION IN DIFFICULT SITUATIONS

Whom Do We Talk to When We Are Hungry, Hurt, Sick, or Afraid?

Overview: The "whom do we talk to when . . ." exercise is conducted to find out about how children deal with difficult situations, and who they trust to help them solve understand their lives.

Description: How do children cope with difficulties in their lives? Who do they talk to when they are hungry, hurt, sick, or afraid? *The purpose of this exercise is to find out who the children trust most when it comes to situations where they need help. With adolescents it can also be used to find out who is the most trusted information provider when they go through body changes.*

Method: This exercise is conducted separately with younger children and adolescents. After rapport has been established with the group, ask them to list the situations in which they seek advice or help from others. This can be done with both school-going and nonschool-going children. More issues can also be added as the children discuss the situations that they face.

Next, ask the children about when the situations first come up. Who do they speak to first? Who is the second person they contact? Note the information in the appropriate columns of the chart as the group reaches consensus for each category.

Expected output: The following diagrams show sample generated output generated from such an exercise:

Young Children (School-going)				
No.	Situation	First contact	Second contact	Remarks
1	Hungry	Mother		
2	Hurt	Mother	Father	
3	Sick	Mother	Father	
4	Afraid	Father	Mother	
5	Not aware of what's happening	Friends	Teacher	
6	Other:			

Adolescents				
No.	Situation	First contact	Second contact	Remarks
1	Body changes (general)	Older siblings	Friends	
2	Body changes (sensitive areas)	Try to read about it	Talk to friends	
3	Difficulty in relationships	Talk to friends		
4	New things happening	Talk to friends	Teacher	If in school
5	Other:			

Analysis and discussion: An analysis of the findings shows that younger children are more likely to talk to their mothers first when they face difficult situations. Their second alternative is usually to contact their father for some of the issues. When it comes to changes taking place in their environment, children who attend school are more likely to first check with their friends and then ask their teacher if they fail to get a suitable answer from their friends. As children grow up and become adolescents, the tendency is more to prefer the company of their peers. It is then the peers who are the main source of information (or often misinformation!) on most issues. For some difficult situations, they may seek the opinions of their teachers as long as they do not feel that this makes them look bad in front of their teachers.

In the picture above, taken during a village meeting in Cambodia, a little boy came to accompany his father while he was attending the meeting. It was a beautiful sight to see the two of them sitting together. The boy tried to figure out what his father found so interesting, and stayed close to him just so that he could continue to interact with him. The little boy was willing to forego the opportunity of playing with his friends just to be with his father. In God's idea, both parents are required to help provide nurture and care for children. However, with the growing poverty in many areas and the all-too-common need for one parent to migrate to earn a living, children are often deprived of the opportunity to receive balanced care and nurture from both of their parents.

FINDING NEW INFORMATION
....

Exercise 26:
INFORMATION ABOUT
COMMUNITY RESOURCES

What Does the NGO Do in Our Community?

Overview: This exercise is conducted to find out how much children know about an NGO or various NGOs working in their community.

Description: This exercise is designed to find out from children what they think a particular NGO that works in the community is doing. *The purpose of the exercise is to find out the children's perspective of the programs and activities of the NGO(s) working in the community, to see to what extent they have been involved in the program-related dialogue.*

Method: After necessary rapport building, ask the focus group of seven- to sixteen-year-old children to explain what types of activities the local NGO is involved in. They might mention construction projects, educational programs, meetings, and more. Once the group has agreed on what they consider to be the main activities of the NGO, have them use the Ten-Seed Technique (TST) to place groups of seeds together for each activity by asking, "What do you think the NGO mainly does?" If there are several NGOs working in the community, make a chart for each of the NGOs that the children think of by themselves without prompting. Also, ask them what they call each NGO.

Expected output: The following diagram shows the output generated from such an exercise:

What Does the NGO Do?		
No.	Activities	Number of Seeds
1.	School building	● ●
2.	Basketball court	● ● ● ●
3.	Water pipes	●
4.	Many meeting with grown-up people	● ● ●

Analysis and discussion: The NGO that was discussed with the children in this particular community was working on a major program and strongly emphasized the integration of child-focused development programs throughout its work. However, the children were not invited to the decision-making meetings and therefore, did not know about all of the programs offered by the NGO within their community.

Major community-level meetings had been organized, involving all the village elders and opinion leaders. Through repeated meetings with them, a

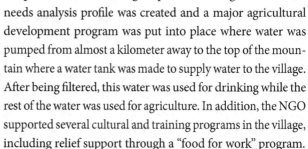

needs analysis profile was created and a major agricultural development program was put into place where water was pumped from almost a kilometer away to the top of the mountain where a water tank was made to supply water to the village. After being filtered, this water was used for drinking while the rest of the water was used for agriculture. In addition, the NGO supported several cultural and training programs in the village, including relief support through a "food for work" program.

After much hard work and a high level of participation of the villagers, it was possible to get funding for road repair, repair and strengthening of field contours, several small microenterprises, healthcare training, and nutrition improvement programs. Even a school building was built, and because the project had some leftover cement, they even made a basketball court. Because the children were never invited, however, they did not know about many of these opportunities, and were left to draw their own conclusions, even about the name of the organization!

CHILDREN'S DREAMS FOR THE FUTURE

Exercise 27:
DREAMS PROFILE A

What Do You Want to Become When You Grow Up?

Overview: This exercise explores the type of future children see for themselves.

Description: This exercise is designed to find out the type of Future children see for themselves in terms of a career. This exercise can be done in the rural areas too, but it is most beneficial to do it in an urban or peri-urban area.

Method: As has been mentioned, this exercise works best with urban or peri urban children. When done with rural children the future career choices are limited to farming and perhaps just one other profession such as becoing a teacher or a doctor. While doing the exercise in the urban (slum) context, all the children to participate are brought out into a central cleared area or inside a large room. Draw a grid on the floor or on a large sheet of paper and ask for volunteers to write down potential future career options as recommended by the group in each box as seen in the example. Children usually recommend only careers that they are familiar with as seen in the example. These are obviously people whom they see on a regular basis in the slum. Ensure that all career options mentioned are listed, leave one box blank with a question mark and give each of the children present a seed. Ask them to hold it tightly in their hand, then hold it close to their head (for a little dramatization), close their eyes shut, think of what they want to be in the future, and then look for the appropriate box and place it there. Pandemonium breaks loose at this time,

Doctor	Lawyer	Teacher	Police Officer	Soldier	Nurse
Trader	Engineer	Electrician	Supervisor	Moneylender	?

with children moving all around excitedly placing the seeds. The facilitator's role at this time is just to ensure that nobody gets hurt and that there is no fighting. After things settle down the children are asked to sit around the 'visual' and a volunteer is asked to make a total of the seeds in each box. Other variations to this exercise consist of using different colored seeds for the boys and girls so that gender variations in career choice can also be observed. After the exercise, it is good to invite people from these 'specifically chosen' careers to come and talk to the children about the type of preperation that is required by them to achieve their dreams. This is particularly important in urban slum areas where children don't get to see good role models. When it it possible to find a professional who has also made it out of a similar poverty affected background, the impact can be spectacular, and serve as a powerful motivator.

Expected output: The output generated for facilitating this exercise will look something like the examples below:

Without gender variation:

Doctor	Lawyer	Teacher	Police Officer	Soldier	Nurse
• • • • •	••••• ••••• •••••	• • • •• • • • •	••••• ••••• ••••	• • • •	•••• •••••

Trader	Engineer	Electrician	Supervisor	Moneylender	?
•	•	• • • •	• •	••••• • • •	• •

With gender variation:

Doctor	Lawyer	Teacher	Police Officer	Soldier	Nurse
◦ ◦ ◦ • ◦	••••• ••••• •••••	◦ • • ◦ ◦ ◦ ◦ ◦	••••• •••• ••••	• • • •	◦ ◦ ◦ ◦ ◦ ◦ ◦ ◦

Trader	Engineer	Electrician	Supervisor	Moneylender	?
•	•	• • • •	• •	••••• • • ◦	• •

Girl: ◦   **Boy:** •

Analysis and discussion: An analysis of the information collected from this exercise show that in urban slums children's choice of career is limited mostly to the type of people they see visiting their community. There is also a sharp difference in terms of gender relation of these career choices. The column with the 'question mark' also got two seeds. When questioned, there was initially silence, and then two little boys spoke up stating that their career was not represted. Turned out that they hadn't spoken up in the begining when the names of potential careers were being prepared, and they didn't know how to portray 'NGO staff' as a career option! These are precautions that should be taken while facilitating the exercise. Ofcourse the box with the question mark is a safe guard to still capture the career options that might get missed.

On one occasion, after completing a similar exercise in one of the cities in India, we found that the career chilce of one of the liitle children was to become a 'Bandit'. Dispite persuasions to change this choice the little boy persisted in wanting to become a bandit. On sensitive investigaton, we finally discovered that it was because he had been abused by a neighbor whom everyone was scared of that he had chosen to grow up and become a gangster to deal with the issue himself! A happy ending to this story is that when the project discovered the problem they were able to use their influence to get the abuser arrested.

* * *

Exercise 28:
DREAMS PROFILE B

What Are Our Hopes for the Future?

Overview: This exercise helps explore the hopes that children have for their future.

Description: This exercise is designed to find out the hopes that children have for their future. As the 'future generation that lives in the present' children represent the future of a community. The hopes that they have for the future show first of all the stability of the community and to what extent it fosters a 'hope for the future'. *The purpose of the exercise is to find out what the children in a community see their future as.*

Method: This exercise is conducted with a mixed gender group of eight to ten children in the seven to fifteen years age group. After rapport has been established with group we use the TST (Ten-Seed Technique) to ask them to show us a profile of how they see their life. This is initially done (as seen in the diagram below) by preparing three columns with three rows below them. The children are indicated that each of the rows represent a stage in their lives —their past, the present, and their future. They are then given the ten seeds and asked to distribute these in the second column. The seeds will often be in larger numbers in the 'past' column and the 'present' column as compared to the future, and care must be taken not to make any suggestive modifications.

After the locations of the seeds have been finalized, the children are asked to describe each of these and the points are noted. Discussions take place around the 'visual' starting with the bottom row (the past) and moving up. When the 'future' column is reached the children are asked to describe what they 'see themselves doing' in it.

Expected output: The following diagram shows the output generated from facilitating such an exercise:

Stage	# of Seeds	Remarks
Future	● ●	Get good jobs in the city Have good farming in the village Have a good life in village to return to from the city every holiday Everyone is very happy and celebrating
Present	● ● ● ●	Parents work very hard the whole year Have good farms and agriculture We study hard in school Listen to parents and obey them Good playground for many games
Past	● ● ● ●	Were very young and dependent on parents and older siblings Did not do very well in studies No good place to play

Analysis and discussion: An analysis of the information generated from facilitating the exercise above shows that the children tend to concentrate more on their past and their present. This is only natural for them because they concentrate on what they have experienced and are experiencing, and the future is often something that is quite remote and unknown. However, as HOPE gets kindled the possibilities of the future emerge as a more real option and they become willing to talk about it. When the 'present' (the current reality) of children is stable and the shadow of uncertainty has passed, children become more interested in thinking about the future. This is when their sceptism about the future passes and they start considering very clear options of the future. This is essentially part of the ideal that all development workers seek to achieve—'giving children a chance to develop their conscience, a hope and a future'. Often times, the facilitation of such an exercise sets the 'ball rolling' as it were, and the children start talking about their future. It is good to encourage this dialogue and hear what they have to say about this. As with the case of the exercise on 'what do you want to become when you grow up', such talks about the future can be promoted by a greater larger discussion with the children of future scenarios that are hopeful. In the case of street children we have often seen that they only start talking about their future when the present stops being uncertain.

* * *

Exercise 29:
DREAMS PROFILE C

Dream Map of Our Village

Overview: This exercise seeks to find out the types of dreams that children have for their village and represent it in a "dream map."

Description: What dreams do children have for their community? Done in a village, urban context, or slum community, *the purpose of this exercise is to find out the future aspirations of the children for their community.*

Method: Identify a group of children to prepare a map of their village on the ground.[66] After a village map is prepared (or alternatively, with the output of the "map of their world"), ask the group of children to point out various places that are important to them. Ask them to think of the future and list some of their dreams for their community and how it might change for the better; then, have them prepare a new map, showing new structures that relate to these changes and dreams. When the "dream map" emerges, ask the children to describe the "new additions" (as compared to the old map) and what these structures are for, including how the children will benefit from them.

....
66   This piece of the exercise is very similar to the "map of their world" exercise. In fact, the output from the "map of their world" can be used as a starting point for the "dream map of our village."

Expected output: The "dream map" will consist of new additions that will be clearly distinguishable from the original map of the village as it exists. There will be tremendous excitement in the faces of the children as they describe the structures in their dream map.

Analysis and discussion: The children's dream map is a helpful profile of the types of developments that children would like to see in their community.

Interestingly, these are usually almost all in the form of structures and buildings that would be useful to the children. Common structures drawn include schools, playgrounds, basketball and volleyball courts, gardens with enclosures, bridges, and roads. Discussions emerging from the review of the map are very important, especially during the preparation of the village resource development plan.[67]

....

67   For more on the village resource development plan, please see Jayakaran, *Participatory Poverty Alleviation and Development.*

* * *

....

Exercise 30:
CREATE YOUR OWN EXERCISE!

Title:

_____

Overview (What does this exercise teach us?):

_____
_____
_____

Description (What is the exercise like? What is its purpose?):

_____
_____
_____

Method (How will the exercise be facilitated?):

_____
_____
_____

(Draw a diagram or paste a photo here.)

Expected output:

<hr>
<hr>
<hr>
<hr>

(Show what the results will look like here.)

<hr>
<hr>
<hr>
<hr>

Analysis and discussion (What can be learned from this exercise?):

<hr>
<hr>
<hr>
<hr>

Section Three

SPECIAL CONSIDERATIONS AND FOLLOW-UP

*   *   *

Lesson 1:
IDENTIFYING CHILD ABUSE

IT IS A joyful and precious privilege to work with children, some of the most sensitive and vulnerable people on earth. Nevertheless, this privilege is at times misused, and these same children become the greatest victims of all sorts of abuses. We live in corrupt societies that are perhaps themselves reeling from past abuse. Ron O'Grady, the author of the powerful book, *The Child and the Tourist*, refers to the treatment of children as a litmus test that measures the quality of a society. Because of its prevalence and impact on children and society, child abuse must be evaluated as one important element of this litmus test.

Scars received in childhood can leave deep psychological wounds that affect children throughout their lives, even into adulthood. It is not the purpose of this book to have an elaborate and detailed lesson on child abuse, but rather, to create awareness. This section will provide some clues regarding how to identify incidents of child abuse and take immediate practical steps to respond.[68]

Child abuse can be categorized into five major types:

1. Neglect
2. Physical abuse
3. Emotional abuse
4. Sexual abuse
5. Commoditization

Let us look briefly at each type.

....

68   For more resources on the subject of child abuse, please see appendix A. In addition, many organizations around the world have made this topic their central focus and have launched programs for the prevention of child abuse. Several of these organizations are also listed.

Neglect

You probably know several neglected children. They can be seen in almost any community on a daily basis. Children experience neglect when their caretakers choose not to provide for their needs of food, clothing, housing, supervision, safe surroundings, healthcare, emotional care, and education.[69] Some children may have been abandoned by their parents or caretakers and left to fend for themselves. Others, despite being with caretakers, still experience neglect because their caretakers either do not understand their needs or their caretakers have other priorities. These other priorities may be the harsh struggle for existence (extreme poverty), or difficulties of coping (single spouse or disability), or the challenges of addiction (substance abuse, such as alcohol or drugs).

The result in most cases is the same. Instead of being cared for, protected, and nourished, the child is deprived of basic nutrition, basic nurture, and basic healthcare. Neglected children are extremely vulnerable to a multitude of risks. In countries with only a limited societal "safety net," many children continue to suffer physically and emotionally for years. In some cases, the damage is permanent—stunted growth, inability to form healthy attachments to other people, and decreased mental abilities are all possible results of neglect.

One of the ways to help neglected children is to link them with an NGO that can help to provide supplementary care while helping parents or caretakers to better understand their role. This way, the children's immediate needs can be taken care of, and the caretakers can also receive support as they learn to take better care of their children.

Physical Abuse

Situations of physical abuse are ones in which the children suffer physical injury. This may happen when a child is punished harshly, even though the intention might not be to hurt the child. When punishment or intentional violence leaves scars, bruises, or marks, this is considered to be physical

....

69 Sometimes, even with loving parents, children may experience these same challenges because of extreme poverty. Neglect, however, occurs when parents have the ability to provide, but choose not to do so. See "Child Neglect," *Psychology Today*, http://psychologytoday.com/conditions/childneglect.html (accessed August 20, 2008).

abuse. Children who have experience physical abuse will often have bruises or marks in the shape of objects or handprints. They may have burn marks, human bite marks, or fractures (usually skull, arms, legs, or ribs). They may have experienced female genital mutilation.[70]

Physically abused children also exhibit behavioral indicators. Examples of these are:

- behavioral extremes, such as aggression, regression, withdrawal, or depression;
- inappropriate or excess fear of parents or caregivers;
- antisocial behavior, such as substance abuse, skipping school, or running away;
- farfetched or inconsistent explanations about injuries; or
- unusual shyness and avoidance of physical contact.

Physical abuse may result in both minor and major injuries, and may even cause lasting damage or even death. Families with a high incidence of domestic violence, or where any of the caregivers are highly stressed, have a high likelihood of experiencing physical abuse. Being vulnerable and helpless, the children often become the "punching bag" in such situations, with the parents venting their anger onto the children. Often, the provocation may be something very simple, but the child ends up getting beaten very badly because the parents are stressed, intoxicated, or angry about other things.

Sometimes, in cases of physical abuse, it has been effective to counsel the families and encourage them to participate as members of a neighborhood watch program where violent behavior is monitored. It is important to immediately connect children with an organization that is geared to working with abused children. Networks can also be effective for prevention and intervention. For example, Vulnerable Children Assistance Organization

....

70   For more on the harmful effects of female genital mutilation (FGM), see UNICEF, "Female Genital Mutilation/Cutting," http://www.unicef.org/protection/index_genitalmutilation.html (accessed February 11, 2009).

(VCAO) in Cambodia has come up with a fairly effective child safety network that uses the children's network to monitor abuse of all kinds.[71]

EMOTIONAL ABUSE

Emotional abuse occurs when caregivers use words to threaten or humiliate children. A visit to the house of such children will usually show parents or caregivers exhibiting highly emotional behavior. They often tend to voice words of rejection toward the child, and their words are often very critical, insulting, humilating, isolating, terrorizing, or corrupting (e.g., swearing in front of the child) for the child. Also, emotionally abusive caregivers tend not to respond to the child emotionally, or they scold the child for exploring their environment.

Emotionally abused children frequently show a variety of physical signs, such as:

- eating disorders, including anorexia or obesity;
- speech disorders, such as stuttering or stammering;
- delays in development related to speech or motor skills;
- subnormal growth; and
- nervous disorders, including rashes, facial tics, stomachaches, and more.

They may also exhibit unusual behaviors like head-banging, rocking, or biting (habit disorders), cruelty toward peers or animals, or a sense of pleasure from being mistreated. Such children also show behavioral extremes, going back and forth between withdrawal and aggression, listlessness and excitability, or overly compliant to demanding behavior.

Many times, it is harder to deal with emotional abuse because there is not enough conclusive evidence—it does not leave a physical mark. Also, caregivers may not realize the damage they are causing, or they may not be willing to admit their guilt. Nevertheless, as in all other cases, the community leaders and concerned NGOs dealing with this issue should be notified.

....

71   See http://www.vcao.org.kh/.

Sexual Abuse

While all forms of abuse are horrible, the most horrible may be sexual abuse. In my opinion, nothing is worse than when a child experiences sexual abuse within the confines of his or her own home. In most of these cases, the child knows the abuser, and the abuser is possibly even part of the extended family. Because of an unequal power relationship, the child is helpless to resist.

Sexual abuse includes fondling, forcing the child to touch the body of the perpetrator inappropriately, penetrative oral, vaginal, or anal sex, indecent exposure to the child, allowing the child to watch pornography, or causing the child to be involved in child pornography and/or sexual exploitation.

Children who have been sexually abused may display physical indicators such as torn, stained, or bloody underclothes. They may have frequent throat or urinary infections, pain and irritation of the genitals, sexually transmitted diseases, or bruises or bleeding from the external genitalia or anal region. Some girls may even become pregnant. Children who have been sexually abused may suddenly tell a peer or adult. They might also act younger than their age, demonstrating regressive behaviors such as thumb sucking, bed-wetting, or fear of the dark. Promiscuity, seductive behavior, disturbed sleep patterns due to recurrent nightmares, unusual and age-inappropriate interest in sexual matters, avoidance of undressing or wearing of extra layers of clothes, sudden decline of academic performance and difficulty in walking or sitting are other symptoms.

As with other forms of abuse, when such abuse is identified, the concerned people in the NGOs dealing with such issues must be notified, and they will advise on further steps. Because of the highly sensitive nature of this form of abuse, the intervention in this case requires a very professional approach so that all necessary links are made for appropriate action.

Commoditization

The word *commoditization* describes the process in which children are gradually seen more and more as commodities. "Children are only important because of their economic value," goes the thinking in this mindset. Persistent, excruciating, and abject poverty can easily lead to this impoverishment of human dignity. Money soon becomes the most important consideration for every situation. Emotions, affection, loyalty, and sex are soon sold for money as part of the survival strategy. In desperation, people who have nothing else left to sell may even then sell off their children for money.

Commoditization happens all over the world. The process usually begins with an exchange of services for an advance of money (child domestic labor or bonded labor). This is called the "push of poverty." In recent years, some have noticed a trend toward the "pull of profit" as well. This occurs when parents desire to purchase luxury goods and the children are either forced to work in order to contribute to family income or sold as a commodity. Rather than receiving care, nurture, and support in preparation for a better future, the children are forced to contribute to the family's financial profit. In my opinion, the "pull of profit" is a far greater and more dangerous trend that will require massive efforts to reverse.

Steps Involved in Dealing with Child Abuse

You and your team must constantly watch for cases of child abuse. In addition, building community awareness on issues of abuse can help the members of the community to identify and deal with child abuse. Communities must be sensitized to the evils of abuse, and they should not just be allowed to be fatalistic or compromising (e.g., making such statements as, "This type of thing commonly happens, we just accept it as the way life is").

More information is available on the subject of child abuse (see appendix A). The following are several initial steps to help you prepare to intervene in cases of abuse:

1. *Identify NGOs to help you.* Identify NGOs in your area or nearby that work for the prevention of child abuse. Invite them to train your staff on how to identify and recognize it. Study their materials. Obtain details of help lines, contact persons, and so on, and keep this information handy.
2. *Develop an organizational action plan.* Either with this organization or on your own, develop an action plan with steps that will be taken when cases of child abuse are identified. Make this information available to all field staff so that they are aware and prepared to respond as they work with the children.

3. *Ensure that all workers are "clean."* Ensure that all staff working with you are legitimate and that no one is an undercover pedophile. Unfortunately, the opportunity to interact with children sometimes attracts the wrong kinds of people.
4. *Take action when cases are identified.* As cases are identified, take action. Use the information, resources, and experts to deal with the issue appropriately. Later, if cases occur frequently, you may need to hire a staff person especially to deal with this issue.
5. *Keep information and resources handy.* Keep information on child abuse available for staff to read through, and whenever possible, invite experts to give talks about identifying and dealing with child abuse. Post rules, help lines, and other key pieces of information for children and staff.

STEPS IN DEALING WITH CHILD ABUSE

1. Identify NGOs to help you.
2. Develop an organizational action plan.
3. Ensure that all workers are "clean."
4. Take action when cases are identified.
5. Keep information and resources handy.

* * *

Lesson 2:
CHILD PROTECTION AND RELATED ADVOCACY ISSUES

EVEN A CURSORY look at the contents of this book will show the reader that it focuses on one important dimension—namely, that children are very precious and that every possible effort must be made to ensure that they grow up in a safe, healthy, and nurturing environment. This environment must be a place where the child is free of any form of discrimination, taken care of by parents or other caretakers, fed, clothed, loved, and respected, and allowed to exercise his or her full rights as a child. In an ideal world, the child will have their identity papers, live a life of safety, and grow up with cultural and religious freedom. Adults who interact with the children must empower them to use their rights and freedoms, including freedom of expression, the right to be heard, the right to participate actively, freedom of association with other groups or organizations, the right to privacy, free access to information, the right to appropriate support if disabled, and the rights to healthcare, education, and secure social status. Each child must have time to grow, play, and have recreation. Not only must the child's rights be guarded but the child must also be protected from all forms of exploitation including drug abuse, kidnapping, trafficking, or armed conflict.

A safe, healthy, and nurturing environment will help the child to grow well, be nourished appropriately, and develop to his or her full potential. Child protection, therefore, is a very serious issue, because we find that most of the children that we interact with live in situations that are very far from this idea.

The following are some of the stages that are important in helping a community become an environment where children are protected and safe:

1. *Teach children about their rights.* The starting point for action is to provide children in the community with a chance to become aware of their rights as children, and to help them understand the implications of their rights in simple terms. With the help of external support, this awareness will help the children to move toward the idea of protecting themselves.

2. *Identify vulnerable children and high-risk areas.* Organizations seeking to work with children must understand the risks that the children face. The organizations need to identify factors that make certain children vulnerable and locations that are potentially dangerous to children. We cannot afford to be naïve on these issues. Identifying vulnerabilities involves research as follows:

   - a review of the existing literature;
   - discussions with child rights advocacy groups in the area; and
   - local research using the Deprivation-Exclusion-Vulnerability Index (DEV Index), described in the next lesson.

3. *Train staff on risks, signs, and policies.* All people who will be working with children must be trained to become aware of the risks that children face and how to recognize signs of abuse. They must also be made aware of your organization's policies for child protection and dealing with abuse. It goes without saying that all such persons must also be screened to ensure that they are "clean" and authentic in the matter of their behavior and motivation for working with children.

4. *Participate in media campaigns to make child abuse a zero tolerance issue.* The media should be motivated and involved so that it regularly addresses the issue of child abuse and seeks to promote an atmosphere where no forms of abuse are tolerated. This can be done by maintaining close contact with the media and providing them with properly researched information so that it can result in better public awareness. In recent years, this has happened extensively in various parts of Asia and there is now considerable public awareness on the issues of sexual exploitation, abuse, and trafficking of children. As a result, people now talk about these issues and are beginning

to make decisions that make their communities better places for children.

5. *Challenge cultural assumptions and traditions.* When victims of child abuse are identified, their stories must be told (with proper masking of their identities, of course), so that the community becomes aware of the devastating impact that abuse has on the life of the child. Communities will learn to talk about these issues, and they will also start challenging their own assumptions and cultural practices. They will begin to question habits that were at one point acceptable to them such as early child marriage, bonded child labor, dedicating girl children as temple prostitutes, and selling children into sexual exploitation. Recently, these issues have come under heavy media scrutiny, and societal attitudes and cultural practices are slowly changing as a result.

STEPS TO CREATE A SAFE ENVIRONMENT FOR CHILDREN

1. Teach children about their rights.
2. Identify vulnerable children and high-risk areas.
3. Train staff on risks, signs, and policies.
4. Participate in media campaigns to make child abuse a zero tolerance issue.
5. Challenge cultural assumptions and traditions.
6. Ensure and establish basic services for rehabilitation.
7. Promote legislation and strong law enforcement.
8. Advocate for the government's commitment to uphold and enforce the law.
9. Advocate where injustice exists.

6. *Ensure and establish basic services for rehabilitation.* When victims are identified, the concerned NGOs will need to ensure that basic rehabilitation services are available. In some cases, this may be in the form of shelters, counseling, or advocacy campaigns. In areas where such services are not available,

some communities and organizations have formed coalitions and divided various roles among the members. This may also sometimes entail specialized training for partners or certain staff members.

7. *Promote legislation and strong law enforcement.* Most countries have laws for child protection. Most have also signed the United Nations Convention on the Rights of the Child and other international protocols to protect children. Sometimes, these are not taken as seriously as they should be. NGOs can play an important role in making legislators aware of their obligations and showing them the kinds of impact that abuse and exploitation have on the lives of children. There are several NGOs in Cambodia that have had a very strong impact, even in the introduction of new laws. The media can play an important role in this as well, especially by helping to identify and highlight non-conformation to laws and international agreements.

8. *Advocate for the government's commitment to uphold and enforce the law.* This is something that takes time to achieve, but will bear fruit as a result of persistent advocacy. Working together as coalitions, partnerships, and networks will add strength and numbers to your efforts. The influence of the local, national, and global media, along with public opinion, will help to increase the government's commitment and enforcement of child protection laws. This stage can lead to a widespread overall impact.

9. *Advocate where injustice exists.* Advocacy is something that the NGO should be involved with on numerous levels. Initially, this will include advocacy and awareness raising at the community level followed by advocacy through the media as issues are identified. Progressively, this move to influence the powerful will move to the provincial, state, national, and perhaps even international levels.

* * *

Lesson 3:
IDENTIFYING AREAS
OF VULNERABILITY USING
THE DEV INDEX

THE DEV INDEX is a way to measure the extent of risk that children in a community face. Study the following diagram:

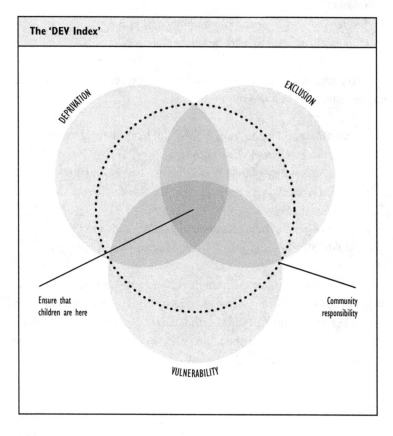

The 'DEV Index'

DEPRIVATION

EXCLUSION

Ensure that children are here

Community responsibility

VULNERABILITY

The three overlapping circles, representing *vulnerability, exclusion,* and *deprivation* are divided into zones as shown in the diagram. The center, where all three overlap, is the ideal place for children to be. The further from the center that a child is, the greater their level of risk. The dotted circle represents the community's responsibility: all children in the community should, at the very least, fit within the dotted circle. The areas outside of the dotted line are those where children are the most deprived, excluded, and vulnerable.

The DEV Index is a participatory tool that can be used for:

- understanding how safe children in a community are;
- finding out the level of risk for exploitation and other challenges;
- identifying the types of risk and the extent to which these exist in the community;
- identifying who is at risk;
- identifying villages and communities at risk; and
- prioritizing areas for early response.

Every society has responsibilities for the younger generations. These responsibilities are in terms of:

- *nourishing* and taking care of their children's physical, social, spiritual, psychological, and other needs;
- *cherishing* and valuing their children so that they are not excluded from the community's care, but able to grow to their full potential; and
- *protecting* their children and their children's rights so that the children are not in a position of vulnerability or exploitation.

Children who are nourished, cherished, and protected are provided for, included, and safe. These are the ones who are (ideally) at the very center of the overlap point of the three circles from the DEV Index diagram. Children who are *not* nourished, cherished, and protected end up deprived, excluded, and vulnerable. They are children at risk.

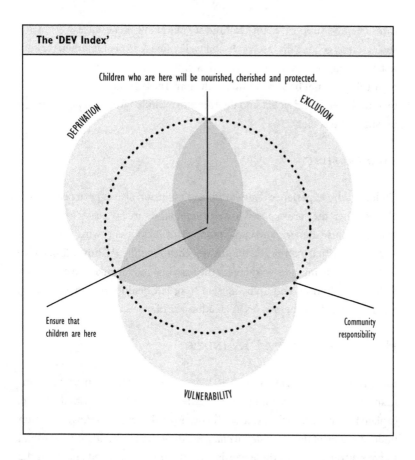

The 'DEV Index'

Children who are here will be nourished, cherished and protected.

DEPRIVATION

EXCLUSION

Ensure that
children are here

Community
responsibility

VULNERABILITY

DEPRIVATION

Children experience deprivation when what rightly belongs to them is taken away. When children are deprived of their human rights, for example, they often do not have their basic needs of nourishment, education, healthcare, shelter, and so on met. Children can also be deprived of the chance to play, learn, and grow. Access to appropriate parental role models at home is another area where many children experience deprivation.

EXCLUSION

Deprivation and exclusion often go hand in hand. Exclusion occurs when caregivers, communities, or societies prevent children from receiving adequate care, love, and support. Many children are marginalized because of ethnicity, social status, gender, disease, or disability. For one reason or another, they are not educated, not treated as well as other children, and not able to develop to their full potential because of this exclusion. These children are deprived of their basic needs and rights, and they are also excluded from full participation in family and society.

VULNERABILITY

Children who experience deprivation and exclusion also experience vulnerability. When they are exposed to a world that they are not ready for, they are at risk of abuse, danger, and exploitation. This includes growing up without any clear spiritual instruction on "the way they should go" (Prov. 22:6). It also includes not having clear warnings of the risks that they are likely to encounter. Vulnerable children end up being sent to or left behind in risky situations, and left to fend for themselves in an adult world.

HOW TO GENERATE A DEV INDEX

Identify a group of eight to ten girls, boys, women, and men from the community who know the community well. After building rapport with the group, explain the purpose of the exercise. Then, ensure that everyone has a common understanding of the terms *deprivation, exclusion,* and *vulnerability*. It is useful to have a translation of these words (and the meanings listed above) in the local language so that when interpretation is done into the local language, the translator can use the words appropriately.

Initiate a Focused Group Discussion (FGD) with the community members. Explain to the group how the Ten-Seed Technique (TST) works, and then ask them to imagine that the ten seeds represent all of the children in the community. Ask the group to distribute ten seeds each for the critical risk factors: deprivation, exclusion, and vulnerability.

Start with ten seeds for one risk factor. For example, when looking at the distribution of children who are deprived, we find that there are three distinct areas where the seeds can be placed: close to the outer rim, within the dotted circle, or in the center of overlap between the three circles. Ask the group to carefully consider all children in the community and then distribute the seeds to show the profile of the entire group. Move on to the next risk factor, placing ten more seeds. You can use seeds of three different colors or look for a different way to be able to see the seeds that were assigned for each risk factor. Finish with the third set of seeds on the final risk factor.

Next, interview the diagram. Ask the group for details about why they distributed the seeds as they did. The following is an example of such a discussion with reasons mentioned in the callouts:

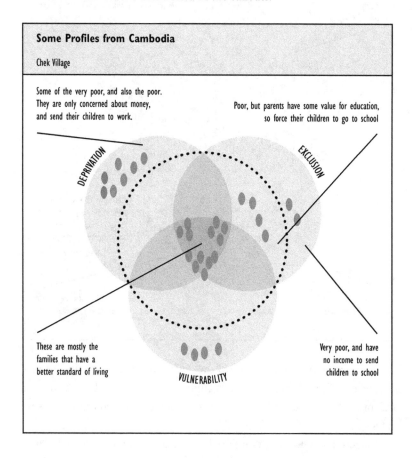

Some Profiles from Cambodia

Chek Village

Some of the very poor, and also the poor. They are only concerned about money, and send their children to work.

Poor, but parents have some value for education, so force their children to go to school

DEPRIVATION

EXCLUSION

These are mostly the families that have a better standard of living

Very poor, and have no income to send children to school

VULNERABILITY

An example of the DEV Index for a group of street children who experience a great number of risks can be seen here:

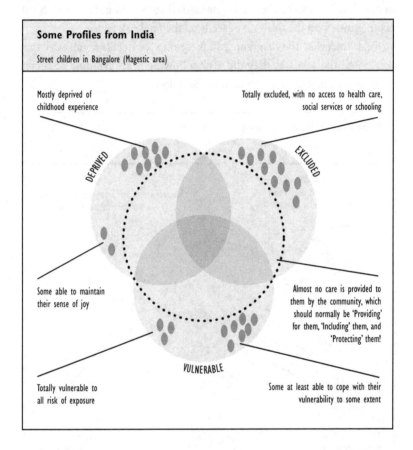

Some Profiles from India

Street children in Bangalore (Magestic area)

Mostly deprived of childhood experience

Totally excluded, with no access to health care, social services or schooling

DEPRIVED

EXCLUDED

Some able to maintain their sense of joy

Almost no care is provided to them by the community, which should normally be 'Providing' for them, 'Including' them, and 'Protecting' them!

VULNERABLE

Totally vulnerable to all risk of exposure

Some at least able to cope with their vulnerability to some extent

By counting the seeds outside of the dotted line, you can count the proportion of children that experience significant risks. The seeds in the overlap area of all three circles will show the proportion of children that experience the fewest risks.

The resultant DEV Index for the Chek Village community would be "thirteen for safety and nine for risk." This shows that not all children experience extreme risks, but a significant number do. For the Bangalore street children, the DEV Index would show "zero for safety and thirty for risk."

In order to go even deeper with this exercise, you can find out more about the region, the risk factors, or the individual children within the community.

To find out more about the region, you can facilitate this exercise with all of the villages or communities in the region. Then, make one list of the communities in order of highest-to-lowest risk level based on the number of seeds outside the dotted line and one list of highest-to-lowest safety level based on the number of seeds in the centermost section of the diagram. Villages or communities that show the highest levels of risk and the lowest levels of safety should be prioritized for interventions, and repeating the exercises at periodic intervals will show if the interventions have been useful or not.

To find out more about the risk factors within a specific community or village, you can go into further details about the types of deprivation, exclusion, and vulnerability that children in the community face. Ask the group to list the types of deprivation in their community. Then, using ten seeds, ask the group to show how the seeds should be divided to illustrate the number of children in each of the categories that they listed. Do this with ten more seeds for exclusion, then ten more for vulnerability. The information from this exercise can help you to plan for appropriate interventions within that village or community.

Another possibility for the DEV Index is using it to find out about actual children who fall into the different sections of the diagram. First, draw a chart like the one below and place ten seeds down each column just like they are distributed in the DEV circle diagram. Then, ask the community members to fill in the names of children who fall into each of the categories: Which children experience the most extreme risks? Which children are the safest? What are the names of the children who experience a medium level of risk?

DEV Index Summary with Names of Children for Chek Village (Date: / /)				
Level of Risk	Deprivation	Exclusion	Vulnerability	List of Children
Extreme Risk	• • • • • • •	• •	• • • •	_____ _____ _____ _____
Medium Risk		• • • •		_____ _____ _____ _____
Safe	• • •	• • • •	• • • • • •	_____ _____ _____ _____

After the chart has been completed, you can facilitate a discussion with the entire group about appropriate strategies for moving children into the "safe" category. Make sure to include the date, so that you can track the movement of individual children to different levels of safety over a period of time. If you realize that children are moving toward positions of greater risk instead of becoming safer, then you will know that you need a radical change in the strategies being used to protect children.

Lesson 4:
ENSURING CHILDREN'S PARTICIPATION THROUGH MONITORING AND EVALUATION BY CHILDREN

THE CHILDREN AND adults in one community identified sixteen areas of concern, four each for "what children are unhappy about," "what children do not like," "what makes children happy," and "uncertainties in children's lives."

The following is the action plan that the community developed:

This is a demonstration of how children can be involved in monitoring and evaluation. Out of the sixteen areas of concern listed on the action plan, the children have to monitor and report progress on eleven. On the right side of the action plan is a schedule for monitoring and evaluation over the course of the year. Encourage the community members to establish a set time in the month for monitoring, perhaps at the beginning of every month or at the middle of every month.

Empowering Children for Monitoring and Evaluation

* * *

When you begin working in a community, very few of the children will have had experience in participating in community decisions, and even fewer will have been involved in monitoring and evaluation. Here are a few tips so that you can help them understand the process and do their best:

- Ask the local NGO for support in getting things started. They might have a meeting place, a series of workshops, or a variety of resources that can be helpful.

- Identify a person that the children's team should report to. The local NGO can play a role in this by identifying a neutral party who is also a part of the village leadership.

- Build the capacity of the children's monitoring team in order to help them fulfill their role effectively.

- Deal seriously with adults who hinder children's participation and refuse to comply with the action plan.

The children's team should consist of a small group of children, both boys and girls, and of varying ages. Encourage them to select a leader. They can take turns or add new members to the group every few months so all children who want to be involved can have a chance to participate.

Alternately, there can be a number of sub-teams that feed information to the main team. While children can manage this team by themselves, they may require some external support to keep things moving. This can be done by the local NGO, the person that the children report to, or another supportive adult.

The children's monitoring team, once identified, can be briefed on its responsibilities and then trained on facilitating the exercises. They should also be shown how to do the necessary documentation of the findings. This documentation should essentially consist of the outputs of the monitoring exercises, which should then be signed by the members.

The children's monitoring team can keep one copy and hand another copy over to the adult representative who they report to. Getting into the habit of keeping records and going through the formality of getting and giving signatures adds an official flavor to the whole process, and children love this feeling of importance and adult-like behavior.

To monitor and evaluate progress, the children will need to be trained on several techniques that can be used to review the progress on that particular issue and determine if there has been improvement or regression as compared to the previous status. There are two main types of monitoring that the children's team will be involved in: 1) incidence reporting; and 2) improvement as compared to status before.

INCIDENCE REPORTING

This will consist of reporting actual occurrences of illness, abuse, noncompliance, and dropping out. For example, when monitoring item 3.A in the action plan, "local NGO with village leaders to work out ways to support extremely poor families to send children to school," the children can report how many children are not attending school, how many children have begun attending school since the last report, and how many children have dropped out of school since the last report. This process of incidence reporting could be especially useful for the community in items 2.B, 3.A, 3.D, and 4.C of the action plan above.

IMPROVEMENT AS COMPARED TO STATUS BEFORE

This will consist of comparing the previous situation with the current situation of the children in the community. For this, the children can use a variety of methods such as the Ten-Seed Technique (as shown below) to see if the situation has improved or worsened. Since the ten seeds are distributed between the two columns of "before" and "current situation," five seeds in each will mean that the situation has remained the same. Fewer seeds in the "current situation" column means a reduction and more seeds in the "current situation" column means an increase.

Progress (Code: _____)		Remarks
Before	Current situation (Date:_____)	

Depending on the situation (if what the children's team is evaluating is a positive or negative behavior), these differences may mean improvements or regressions. For example, the children's team can discuss item 2.D of the action plan, "parents to try not to give tasks to children just to keep them busy" to evaluate if the situation has grown worse, remained the same, or improved. If parents have succeeded in giving fewer "busywork" tasks, there will be fewer seeds in the "current situation" column, which will show how much the situation has improved over time. In the action plan above, this methodology will apply to items 1.B, 1.C, 1.D, 2.D, 3.B, 3.C, 4.C, and 4.D.

For the first few times when this evaluation is done, the local NGO will have to guide the children through the process. Once it is certain they can manage on their own, they should be left to do it by themselves.

INVOLVING CHILDREN IN GENERAL MONITORING AND EVALUATION

Part of mobilizing children's participation is empowering their involvement in the monitoring and evaluation of the child participation plan.[72] Another part is involving children in the overall general monitoring and evaluation of programs or projects that are designed to assist the entire community. While making impact assessments, you can carefully and simply explain the program objectives so that they can also share their feedback in terms of how their lives were impacted.

For example, if the family says that because of one of the programs their household income has increased, you could ask the children in that home about the ways in which the new income has made a difference in their lives. This is

....
72   See section 3, lesson 6.

very important in organizations that have a child-focused development objective. It also encourages dialogue between children and parents and promotes discussions about the ways that each family member has benefited.

Before involving children in this process, the evaluation team members will have to figure out the types of questions that they will ask children for each of the impact objectives. The questions must be simple and related to the interests of the children.

Code	Issue	Action	Action By	Deadline for Achievement											
				January	February	March	April	May	June	July	August	September	October	November	December
I.A	What Children Are Unhappy About	Parents to keep younger children with them	Parents	●	●										
I.B		Expectations from children to be realistic and properly explained	Parents	●	●	●	●	●	●	●					
		Children to work harder to learn basics of Meao language	Children		●	●	●	●	●						
I.C		Parents must explain why they cannot buy everything that the children ask for (and also not just refuse everything)—encourage dialogue	Parents	●	●										
		Children to become responsible and not make unreasonable demands on parents	Children	●	●	●									
I.D		Parents to come up with an optimum solution regarding expectations from children on learning both Mandarin and basics of Meao language	Parents	●	●	●									
		After parents come up with expectations, children to make special attempts to learn at least basics of Meao language	Children			●	●	●	●	●	●	●	●	●	●

Code	Issue	Action	Action By	\multicolumn{12}{c}{Deadline for Achievement}											
				January	February	March	April	May	June	July	August	September	October	November	December
2A	What Children Do Not Like	Adults to be more sensitive about the "shouting and fighting"	Adults with help from NGO	●	●										
2B		Village leaders to form action group to stop the cutting of trees and plucking of flowers	Adults	●	●	●	●	●	●	●	●	●	●	●	●
		Children's group to be formed to give feedback to adult action group on cutting of trees and plucking of flowers	Children		●	●									
2C		Appropriate solution to be determined by village leaders and NGO for problem relating to "grazing supervision" by children	Village leaders and local NGO	●	●	●	●	●	●						
2D		Parents to try not to give tasks to children just to keep them busy	Parents	●											
		Children's team to monitor progress	Children		●	●	●		●		●		●		●

Code	Issue	Action	Action By	Jan	Feb	Mar	Apr	May	Jun	Jul	Aug	Sep	Oct	Nov	Dec
3.A	What Makes Children Happy	Local NGO with village leaders to work out ways to support extremely poor families to send children to school	Local NGO and village leaders	●	●	●		●		●		●		●	
		Monitor school dropouts and children not going to school	Children's team			●									
3.B		Share more house responsibilities with children	Parents	●	●	●	●	●							
		Facilitate sessions for parents on the role of play in the life of a child	NGO staff	●			●						●		
		Monitor progress	Children's team	●											
3.C		Parents to be more sensitive about how serious games are to children	Parents	●	●	●	●●	●	●	●		●			●
		Monitor progress	Children's monitoring team	●	●		●								
3.D		All parents to encourage starting a flower plot near their house	Parents		●	●	●	●						●	
		Monitor progress	Children's monitoring team	●●	●●	●●		●●		●		●			

Code	Issue	Action	Action By	Jan	Feb	Mar	Apr	May	Jun	Jul	Aug	Sep	Oct	Nov	Dec
4.A	Uncertainties in Children's Lives	Parents to be more sensitive to how important games are for their children	Parents	●	●	●	●								
		Local NGO to have sessions for parents on the importance of play for children	Local NGO	●	●	●	●								
4.B		Local NGO and health department to identify and treat problems related to high incidence of waterborne disease	Local NGO, village elders, and health department	●	●	●									
		Monitoring of disease incidence	Children's monitoring team						●	●		●		●	
4.C		Bring improvement and stability to agriculture	Local NGO with village elders	●	●	●	●	●	●	●	●	●	●	●	●
4.D		Avoid losing temper	Parents	●	●	●	●	●	●	●	●	●	●	●	●
		Monitoring incidence of anger-abuse in the community	Children's monitoring team	●	●	●			●			●			●

* * *

Lesson 5:
CARRYING OUT A CAPACITY/ VULNERABILITY ANALYSIS USING THE HOLISTIC WORLDVIEW ANALYSIS FRAME

THE HOLISTIC WORLDVIEW Analysis (HWVA) frame can help you to understand children's worldview, and the Capacity/Vulnerability Analysis can help you to understand their ability to make changes in their situations. The HWVA frame's usefulness in analyzing the worldview of a community has been extensively documented in poverty reduction and development programs. We will look now at specific ways that this participatory tool can be used with children, especially as it relates to the development of a plan for child participation within the community.

Using information from four of the exercises,

- Problem Analysis A: What We Are Unhappy About (exercise 17),
- Problem Analysis B: What We Don't Like (exercise 17),
- Blessing Analysis: Things That Make Us Happy (exercise 18), and
- Uncertainty Analysis: Things We Are Unsure About (exercise 19),

collect the outputs together as shown in this example from a community from a minority people group in southwest China:

What They Are Unhappy About	
They don't get to sleep well at night	• •
Being beaten and scolded by parents	• •
When parents don't buy them the things they want	• • •
Getting poor results in school	• • •

What They Don't Like	
Don't like fighting and shouting	• • • • • •
Cutting trees and plucking flowers	• •
Grazing cows	•
Wandering about	•

What Makes Them Happy	
Going to school	● ● ● ●
Doing housework	● ● ●
Playing	● ●
Planting flowers	●

Uncertainty Analysis	
Parents stop children from playing without warning	● ● ● ● ●
Sudden additional chores during school holidays	● ● ●
Illness	●
Crop failure or low harvest	●

The children identified four issues for each of these exercises, for a total of sixteen issues. This means that along with the standard three concentric circles, a total of sixteen segments will be required for the HWVA frame as shown in the diagram below.

The three concentric circles represent various levels of control exhibited by different people. The innermost circle represents the areas of control that the children are able to assert over a particular issue. The middle circle represents the areas where parents and other adults have control. The outermost circle represents aspects of the issue over which neither the community nor the adults have control.

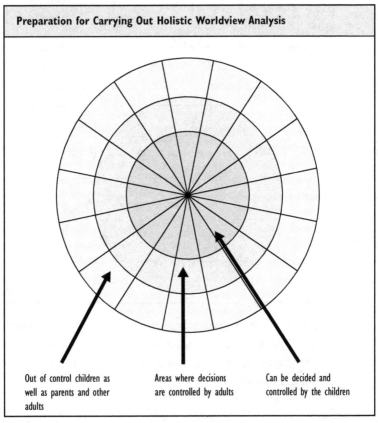

Preparation for Carrying Out Holistic Worldview Analysis

Out of control children as well as parents and other adults

Areas where decisions are controlled by adults

Can be decided and controlled by the children

HWVA for children/Ravi Jayakaran

List each of the sixteen issues next to the segments in the diagram, one for each. Then, use the Ten-Seed Technique (TST) for each of the issues to determine what the status of control and influence is for each. The outcome of this will look something like the following diagram:

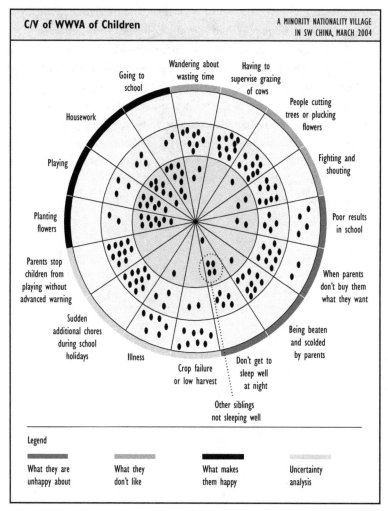

C/V of WWVA of Children

A MINORITY NATIONALITY VILLAGE
IN SW CHINA, MARCH 2004

Going to school
Wandering about wasting time
Having to supervise grazing of cows
Housework
People cutting trees or plucking flowers
Playing
Fighting and shouting
Planting flowers
Poor results in school
Parents stop children from playing without advanced warning
When parents don't buy them what they want
Sudden additional chores during school holidays
Being beaten and scolded by parents
Illness
Crop failure or low harvest
Don't get to sleep well at night
Other siblings not sleeping well

Legend

| What they are unhappy about | What they don't like | What makes them happy | Uncertainty analysis |

WWVA for children/Ravi Jayakaran

In the above Capacity/Vulnerability Analysis, we see the degrees of control that children and adults exercise in each of the sixteen areas that concern children. The diagram above has a color code that makes this quite clear. While all sixteen areas need to be addressed, the first priority areas are the ones with seeds in the outermost circle, followed by the ones that are high in the second row.

Children can be involved in the follow-up actions related to this analysis through a carefully prepared Child Participation Plan. The ultimate purpose of this is not merely to be able to give more control to the children, but to enable the process of healthy, interactive dialogue between all stakeholders (children, parents, and other adults) to understand why a particular perception or situation exists and then work toward remedying it. With dialogue children can better understand the reasons why their parents are opposed to particular actions. At the same time, children are able to explain some of their concerns and grievances related to how they feel about their parents' decisions. Children's participation helps families to become more open about these matters and to understand one another more clearly.

Lesson 6:
PREPARING THE COMMUNITY'S CHILD PARTICIPATION PLAN

AFTER CARRYING OUT the Holistic Worldview Analysis (HWVA) and the Capacity/Vulnerability Analysis, you will have the tools that you need to develop a Child Participation Plan for the community.

You will use the same exercises (exercises 17, 18, and 19), the issues that arose from each, and the distribution of seeds that was determined during the Capacity/Vulnerability Analysis. To these pieces, you will add four new columns: *Remarks*, *Action to be Taken*, *Action By*, and *Deadline*. As you discuss the ways that children will be involved and the changes that the community wants to see, you can fill in these four columns. The *Remarks* column is a place where you can write down notes about what people said, how people feel, or details about the actions that will be taken. The *Action to be Taken* column describes what will be done, while the *Action By* column explains who will do it. Finally, the *Deadline* is when the community decides that the action should be completed by. This may be a month, several months, or more.

Using the same information from the Capacity/Vulnerability Analysis, the first part of the Child Participation Plan would look like this:

Code	Issue	Action	Action By	January	February	March	April	May	June	July	August	September	October	November	December
								Deadline for Achievement							
I.A	What Children Are Unhappy About	Parents to keep younger children with them	Parents	●	●										
I.B		Expectations from children to be realistic and properly explained	Parents	●	●	●	●	●	●						
		Children to work harder to learn basics of Meao language	Children		●	●	●	●	●	●					
I.C		Parents must explain why they cannot buy everything that the children ask for (and also not just refuse everything)—encourage dialogue	Parents	●	●										
		Children to become responsible and not make unreasonable demands on parents	Children	●	●										
I.D		Parents to come up with an optimum solution regarding expectations from children on learning both Mandarin and basics of Meao language	Parents	●	●	●									
		After parents come up with expectations, children to make special attempts to learn at least basics of Meao language	Children			●	●	●	●	●	●	●	●	●	●

222

Part two would look as follows:

Code	Issue	Action	Action By		Deadline for Achievement										
				January	February	March	April	May	June	July	August	September	October	November	December
2A	What Children Do Not Like	Adults to be more sensitive about the "shouting and fighting"	Adults with help from NGO	●	●										
2B		Village leaders to form action group to stop the cutting of trees and plucking of flowers	Adults	●	●	●									
		Children's group to be formed to give feedback to adult action group on cutting of trees and plucking of flowers	Children		●	●	●	●	●	●	●	●	●	●	●
2C		Appropriate solution to be determined by village leaders and NGO for problem relating to "grazing supervision" by children	Village leaders and local NGO	●	●	●	●	●	●						
2D		Parents to try not to give tasks to children just to keep them busy	Parents	●	●										
		Children's team to monitor progress	Children		●	●	●		●		●		●		●

223

Part three would look as follows:

Code	Issue	Action	Action By	Jan	Feb	Mar	Apr	May	Jun	Jul	Aug	Sep	Oct	Nov	Dec
3.A	What Makes Children Happy	Local NGO with village leaders to work out ways to support extremely poor families to send children to school	Local NGO and village leaders	●	●	●									
		Monitor school dropouts and children not going to school	Children's team			●		●		●		●		●	
3.B		Share more house responsibilities with children	Parents	●	●	●	●	●							
		Facilitate sessions for parents on the role of play in the life of a child	NGO staff	●											
		Monitor progress	Children's team	●			●			●			●		
3.C		Parents to be more sensitive about how serious games are to children	Parents	●	●	●	●	●							
		Monitor progress	Children's monitoring team						●						●
3.D		All parents to encourage starting a flower plot near their house	Parents	●	●	●	●	●							
		Monitor progress	Children's monitoring team	●	●	●		●		●		●		●	

Part four would look as follows:

Code	Issue	Action	Action By	Jan	Feb	Mar	Apr	May	Jun	Jul	Aug	Sep	Oct	Nov	Dec
4.A	Uncertainties in Children's Lives	Parents to be more sensitive to how important games are for their children	Parents	●	●	●	●								
		Local NGO to have sessions for parents on the importance of play for children	Local NGO	●	●	●	●								
4.B		Local NGO and health department to identify and treat problems related to high incidence of waterborne disease	Local NGO, village elders, and health department	●	●	●			●	●					
		Monitoring of disease incidence	Children's monitoring team							●		●		●	
4.C		Bring improvement and stability to agriculture	Local NGO with village elders	●	●	●	●	●	●	●	●	●	●	●	●
4.D		Avoid losing temper	Parents	●	●	●	●	●	●	●	●	●	●	●	●
		Monitoring incidence of anger-abuse in the community	Children's monitoring team	●	●	●			●			●			●

225

The action plan is simple and straightforward, and it can either be prepared as a separate document or left as it is above and acted on with this document as a reference.

> If you list the issues in the same order on the Capacity/Vulnerability Analysis and the Child Participation Plan, this can help to make the diagrams more understandable. It can also help the community to prioritize issues that need to be acted on first.
>
> It is also important to keep the deadlines short and ensure that some things are acted on immediately. This will ensure that the children can clearly see changes taking place in their community. As results continue to be progressively achieved, their level of patience will also increase for the things that take a little longer.

Being involved in events in the community that involve healthy interfaces with adults can give children a sense of importance and self-worth. It is the right foundation for building and developing a sense of responsibility for the

community's natural resources and infrastructure. After all, the children are the rightful heirs of all of this. As the children's responsibility grows, there will also be a growing sense of responsibility and accountability on the part of their parents' generation to recognize that they are merely custodians of these resources, using them with a sense of responsibility before handing them over to the next generation who are the rightful owners.

Children's struggles are quite realistic and they want to be treated with respect when it comes to decisions that relate to their lives. Many of these struggles can be eased or solved entirely when they are able to dialogue with adults and understand the logic behind the adults' decisions. For issues where neither children nor parents have much control—like low crop yields—long-term interventions will probably be required. In such issues, the timely intervention of local NGOs is very important.

Since the process of analyzing worldview, analyzing capacity, and developing a Child Participation Plan is often only possible when there is an external NGO in the area, you will need to make sure that they will also commit to the Child Participation Plan and perform some of the follow-up actions.

It is also good to regularly monitor progress and give feedback from the community's Child Participation Plan to the children and adults of the community. I would encourage you to especially celebrate times of achieving milestones and honor those who have achieved great strides of improvement.

Conclusion

By now, I hope that you are convinced about the essential role that child participation plays and can play in the community development process. By ignoring children and their active participation, or by replacing it with paternalistic assumptions where we presume to know what children need and want, we do immense harm to the community. This book makes a strong statement that children are important now and also for the future. They are critical stakeholders in the community. Therefore, we cannot ignore them or their active participation and views. The call goes out to embrace an attitude of humility that seeks to truly listen to the voices of children.

If this is a step that you are willing to take, then there is much that you can learn from this book and adapt in your daily work. The book is full of easy-to-use tools that you can keep referring back to as you develop your own creative and innovative tools that fit your context.

Writing this book has been a long process. Before starting, I talked with several field practitioners from child-focused development organizations about the types of struggles that they had in the field, and the types of information that would be most useful for them. I also observed many things during my own field visits. Based on these discussions and observations, the list of topics was prepared. Additional practitioners then shared their wish lists with me and the final outline gradually emerged.

It has been a very satisfying experience to work on this book and share ideas on a wide range of issues. Some of them have been discussed in detail, while others have just been mentioned briefly. More information is available on a number of topics, and I hope that you will also be able to adapt the materials here to fit your needs.

I encourage all those who read this book to start using the techniques yourself, even if you are not a field practitioner. As you use the book, do also give me feedback on emerging issues that you may encounter.

Dr. Ravi Jayakaran
Ravi@Jayakaran.com
RJayakaran@map.org
www.ravijayakaran.com

∗ ∗ ∗

Appendix A:
THE TEN-SEED TECHNIQUE

THE TEN-SEED TECHNIQUE (TST) is a tool based on and modified from Participatory Learning and Action (PLA) concepts.[73] It was introduced after much modification and experimentation as a tool that can be used to carry out PLA exercises. It is useful in gathering qualitative information on various issues, especially related to the perceptions of the community and the way people see themselves in relation to others. The technique is very flexible and therefore versatile, enabling its use in combination with other techniques and for collecting a wide range of information.

The TST enables probing deeply into different dimensions of an issue, for carrying out what is referred to as a process of opening up the information. This essentially involves going deeper into an issue after starting at the absolute basic level. For example, we find out about the health status of a community and then go deeper into it to find out reasons for differences among various community members, link this information with their economic status, and go further into exploring the types of healthcare that each group is able to access. This opening up process can keep continuing as we find links to levels of education, attitudes, and more.

PHILOSOPHY BEHIND THE TECHNIQUE

This technique relies on using the right brain function so that the full potential of the brain for perceptive analysis is utilized. The right brain is initiated into

....
73   For more information, please visit http://www.fao.org/Participation/ft_show.jsp?ID=1981.

action by visuals such as pictures and three-dimensional items. When we use seeds to depict aspects of information, the visual created by the seeds (strong contrast of colors between the seeds and background), helps the right brain play a dominant role in the analysis.

When this technique was first developed, it was designed to empower illiterate villagers to participate in discussions related to analyzing their situation. The idea was to remove differences due to literacy and enable those without literacy to be able to participate equally with those who were literate. However, when the technique was used, we discovered that there were additional benefits from the activation of the right brain. The right brain controls creativity, spatial awareness, and visual perception. It also has access to the information in both the left brain and the subconscious mind. Thus, using the TST employs both sides of the brain. Because of this, the technique is now used with children and adults, literate and illiterate.

How the Technique Works

First, build rapport with the group and explain to them that the purpose of the exercise is to understand and learn from them about their perspectives. Next, give the group ten seeds and explain that the seeds represent the entire population under study (e.g., all children in the community, all income for one year, all activities during the rainy season, etc.). Then ask the group to move the seeds around into categories. Once the categories have been determined, ask the participants to describe each category and give details about their reasons for classifying the seeds as they have. Ask questions to reveal further details and indicators that determined the categories.

Percent of Population Using Birth Control Measures Regularly	
Use	Don't Use

Each group of seeds will now have a very distinct identity given to it by the participants, and discussions can now proceed around the visual that has been created. Discussions around the visual often become very intense and animated. After finalizing the categories and distribution of seeds, transfer the information onto paper for sharing with the larger community or group.

After this is done, we proceed further to ask more details. For example, if we initially asked about the proportion of the population in the community that use or do not use birth control, then we would find out more details by asking about the types of birth control measures that are used. You can do this by asking the group to look at the visual, pointing to the eight seeds that represent the population that regularly practices birth control measures, and asking the group to divide this population further in terms of the types of measures practiced.

This can be done in two ways, either 1) just asking them to divide the eight seeds; or 2) by again taking ten seeds and asking the group to use these seeds to represent those who practice family planning measures regularly. Thus, it is possible to identify approximately what percentage of the overall population uses each particular type of birth control measure. In the example above, we found that the community was under the perception that they were quite well protected against HIV and AIDS because a fairly high percentage of them were using birth control measures. They had, in their thinking, equated protection against pregnancy as being protected against HIV and AIDS. Discussions around the visual then could proceed to understand why this was so. Thus, the exercise enabled us to see that only 30 percent of the birth control measures in use were condoms (which also did not provide them 100 percent protection against the spread of HIV and AIDS).

Type of Birth Control Measures Adapted				
Sterilization	Pills	IUD (Intra Uterine Device)	Condom	Natural Family Planning
●	● ● ● ●	●	● ● ●	●

You will find that many times, these exercises can form the basis of community discussions about ways that they need to change as they discover how many risks they face. They are not just being informed, they are participating, and so they often care very much about the outcomes. These discussions can also lead to understanding appropriate interventions in the community to change behavior. Other exercises can be linked to this to find out how the community gets its information and thus we can identify the best and most effective strategy for intervening in the community.

GROUP SIZE AND PARTICIPATION

The ideal number of participants in a group is eight to ten people. Keep in mind that these optimum numbers may not always be possible in the community, and the group may sometimes need to be smaller or larger. In larger groups, the actual number of active participants may only be eight to ten. If the group is too large, you might want to split them into several groups.

Giving everyone an equal chance to share views can enable active participation. Sometimes, it may be necessary to filter out the overly dominant participants in the group so that others can participate. This can be done diplomatically by having one of your team members invite the person to another area for a key informant interview. This has the double benefits of seeing the rest of the group become more active in participation and also obtaining important information from the person who was filtered out. Prime candidates for this type of filtering are usually teachers, village chiefs, businesspeople, moneylenders, and educated people in illiterate communities.

FACILITATING THE EXERCISES

It is important to get the group used to working with each other before they start working in the community. Besides establishing a code of conduct to respect and value one another, group members must also decide roles among themselves to determine who will be the interviewer, the recorder, and (if the situation calls for it) the filter.

Developing openness to new perspectives, ideas, and views is essential. One has to seek to listen and learn (not seek to confirm predetermined ideas). Success is almost guaranteed if you can develop a listening attitude. A good facilitator is sensitive to the local context and culture, ensures equal participation for all members of the group, and counters dominance by individuals trying to become spokespersons for the group. If handled correctly, the exercises will generate animated discussions among the participants. Let facilitation become a way of life for you, not only at work, but also in your personal life!

As with other PRA/PLA exercises, healthy facilitation also ensures that there is a balance between being open to new and divergent views as well as being focused enough to lead the discussions in the direction of the information being sought. Additionally, the facilitator (interviewer) should also keep track of the time required for the exercise so that it neither hurries nor drags on too long.

> For best results, facilitation must aim at getting the group to move the seeds first, then describe the category instead of preparing a list first and then trying to force the seeds to fit in the slots.

ASKING GOOD QUESTIONS

A foundational principle to remember in asking questions is to ask questions to learn and understand, not to affirm presupposed assumptions. Therefore, questions that are asked should be open-ended. The 5W+1H (Who? What? Where? When? Why? +How?) Principle is a good one to adapt. The general principle is to start with the simplified foundational information first, and then get deeper and deeper into the issue. Going deeper into issues to open up the information is a little more complex but comes easier with practice. Here, too, the best results are obtained by continuing to be as visual as possible and getting participants to move the seeds first and then describe the categories.

INTERVIEWING THE VISUAL

Once the seeds have been placed in different categories, review the resulting visual with the participants to make sure that everyone understands the placement of the seeds. After this, you can discuss various aspects of the visual, called interviewing the visual. This is a very non-threatening method, as you can look at the visual instead of having to make direct eye contact with the participants. This is especially helpful when collecting sensitive information, as some participants may feel embarrassed if you look directly at them. When they feel comfortable and they are ready for it, they will often make eye contact, but this is usually based on an established relationship. At the end of the session, invite a participant from the community to give a summary of the observations and findings. The visual can be copied and the original left behind for use by the community members in future.

Opening Up the Information

Opening up the information can help you to delve deeper into details from the exercise. For example, if you have facilitated an exercise about the food security status of a village, you can delve deeper into the details of how the food security status relates to patterns of migration by finding out about the level of children's education, health status, migration patterns, uses of different programs, and more for each food security status level.

Although carrying out this exercise may result in a complicated diagram, it will help your team to understand the ramifications and underlying issues involved. Since the complex diagram emerged from the simple, it will be easier to understand, describe, and discuss for all participants, even the villagers with low or no literacy.

Using the Information

Information generated by using the TST must be used as soon as possible in planning and designing processes. However, what often happens is that those who collect the information are unable to analyze it, and thus, do not know how to use it. Depending on the purpose of the exercise, there is a variety of ways to analyze and use the information.

When using the technique for analyzing specific issues, such as the level of vaccination, you can use the results of the TST to find out specific children that have not been vaccinated, and then generate a plan of action for getting the unvaccinated children vaccinated.

Sometimes, an exercise is done to identify the causes of a specific problem. The information that is generated can immediately be used by addressing the identified causes within the family, NGO, or community. The participants of the exercise can be asked how to ensure that this happens for each level identified so that a plan for monitoring and evaluation also begins to take shape.

On other occasions, an exercise is done to find out why a particular program is not succeeding. The approach here would be to make modifications as suggested by the community. The progress of the program against planned objectives can be noted in the form of an evaluation. For example, if the planned impact for a particular objective was "x" and we represented this with ten seeds, we would then ask the community how many seeds would represent the actual impact that the program has already had. If the group placed seven seeds in the "actual impact" column and three seeds in the "improvement" column, we would ask

them to list the things that the seven seeds represented and then list the ways that the program needs to improve in order for the final three seeds to move over to the "actual impact" column.

For more detailed purposes, the results of several different exercises can be combined for analysis and action. For example, they can prepare a problem analysis, livelihood analysis, and uncertainty profile for the Holistic Worldview Analysis (HWVA), which, in turn, can be used to generate a capacity/vulnerability analysis. The final results can then be examined to determine what types of training, intervention, or advocacy would be most effective for the community.[74]

PRECAUTIONS AND POTENTIAL CHALLENGES

Several precautions are important while using the Ten-Seed Technique. The first and most important is that the facilitator must have the correct attitude. This is mandatory. Second, the purpose of the exercise must be clearly explained to the community at the very beginning. Since the technique uses right-brain function, it has the potential to bring hopes and dreams to the surface, so something must be done to address these after the exercise. Similarly, when seeking sensitive information, it may throw light on an exploitative situation in the village that

....

74   When the entire series of exercises is conducted, you can also use the information to create a Village Resource Development Plan (VRDP). For more information on this, please see Jayakaran, *Participatory Poverty Alleviation and Development*.

must be dealt with right away. If situations are not dealt with soon, they will result in frustration and the oppression may continue unchecked.

One potential problem that can hinder good participation from the community is the presence of overly dominant people in the group. To deal with this, filter out dominators for key informant interviews as mentioned previously. Other problems can be avoided by being sensitive to the presence of people with vested interests in the group and ensuring that information is not biased in favor of their interests. Gender-biased information should be countered by trying to ensure that there is a balance of genders in the group, or by facilitating the exercise once with males and once with females. If the context is one in which women will hesitate to speak in the presence of men, then divide the participants into two groups. Choose the timing for the exercises carefully so that they disrupt the normal life of the community as little as possible and so that as many participants as you need will be available.

Key Success Factors

The correct attitude, a balanced team, adequate time, and the ability to keep the group working with a right-brain orientation are some of the key success factors in obtaining quality information. The "outsiders" carrying out the Ten-Seed Technique exercises in the community must have a positive, listening, and open attitude. They must be open to new perspectives and views without presupposed assumptions that merely need an affirmation from the community. A balanced team with varied experience and the ability to listen and work together without trying to dominate team members or members of the community is also important. Such a team will be able to empower the community to participate meaningfully and spontaneously. Adequate time should be available so that there is no need to rush. The exercise can then be coordinated and facilitated well, and can focus on good discussions with openness to new views and perspectives. It is also very important to keep the group working with a right-brain orientation, using visuals, symbols, and diagrams, especially at the beginning of each new exercise.[75]

....
75   To emphasize the right brain as much as possible, I recommend *only* using visuals, symbols, and diagrams at first, and then adding text later.

Advantages of the Technique

The TST is very simple to learn and understand. It is also easy to practice. It has been tested in many different cultures, among people of various social classes, genders, and ages, and it has worked effectively in all of them.

Another advantage is that seeds are easily available in most places. They are very non-threatening, and they are easy to move again and again. Once the moving around of seeds stops with unanimous agreement, the information can be written on a sheet of paper to be saved, filed, and used.

The technique is a very visual one, and because of this, it allows for the literate and illiterate to participate as equal partners and contribute meaningfully to the discussion. The specific number of seeds enables the group to make reasonable comparisons, and the information can be used to determine approximate percentages. The resultant visuals are easy to explain, understand, and discuss.

Additional Potential Uses of the Technique

As has been already mentioned, the TST can be used to collect information for a variety of exercises including level of risk, patterns of distribution among a population (healthcare, disease incidence, birth control practices, etc.), and many other issues that project staff need to collect information about. Besides these, several of the routine PLA exercises can also be carried out using this technique. For example, trends analysis, seasonality diagram, livelihood analysis, expenditure analysis, problem analysis, and more can make use of the TST. Some of the newer exercises, including Holistic Worldview Analysis (HWVA), capacity/vulnerability analysis, rapid food security status assessment (RFSSA), gender desegregation, HIV and AIDS macro zoom, and district- or county-level planning can also use the TST. These additional exercises have been designed because of specific needs in program management and other community needs. A number of examples are included in the lessons and exercises in this book, such as:

- *Household Food Security Status* (see section 1, lesson 3)
- *Trends Analysis* (see exercise 3)

- *Seasonal Activities* (see exercise 14)[76]
- *Problem Analysis* (see exercise 17)
- *Holistic Worldview Analysis* (see section 3, lesson 5)

The technique can also be used and adapted for a variety of additional exercises, including:

- *Livelihood Analysis*: Ask the group to imagine that the ten seeds represent the entire income of the whole village from all sources for an entire year. To make it easier, you can ask them to imagine that all goods, services, and materials that they receive are converted into money as well. Then, ask them to divide the seeds into groups representing the sources of the income in order to find out what their main livelihood sources are.
- *Expenditure Analysis:* Ask the group to imagine that the ten seeds represent the total expenditures of the village for the whole year. Then, ask them to group the seeds into clusters to show what those various expenditure categories are on a yearly basis. Again, this will allow you to determine the percentage of expenditures on various items such as food, clothes, medical treatment, and so on.
- *Disease Incidence:* Ask the group to imagine that the ten seeds represent all the diseases that occur in the village throughout the year. The numbers of seeds in each group show us the percentages for each type of disease in a year.
- *Gender Desegregation:* This exercise is carried out to identify issues that are gender-related and to determine who makes decisions in the family and in the community. For example, if family planning comes up as an issue that is different among men and women, then ask the group what extent of the decision on family planning is determined by the men and what extent by the women.

....

76   The group is asked to carry out a seasonality diagram as in the standard practice, but with the change that for each of the seasonal events such as rainfall, agriculture, disease incidence, festivals, labor opportunities, etc., they are asked to use only ten seeds for each. This will enable you to identify the occurrences according to percentage of intensity at different times of the year.

CONCLUSION

The Ten-Seed Technique is simple and useful. It can help you to understand specific details about a community, analyze and evaluate situations and programs, and develop plans for implementation and monitoring. Perhaps most importantly, the Ten-Seed Technique can also help you to empower the community to act on their findings, making healthy choices and positive changes for the future.

* * *

Appendix B:
RESOURCES

General Books and Articles

Brewster, Dan. *Child, Church and Mission.* Compassion International, 2005.

Chambers, Robert. *Ideas for Development.* London: Earthscan, 2005.

Hope, Anne and Sally Timmel. *Training for Transformation: A Handbook for Community Workers.* Vol. 4. London: Intermediate Technology Publications Ltd., 2000.

Jayakaran, Ravi. *Stories of Transformation: Experiences of Transformation from Development Work,* 2006.

May, Scottie, Beth Posterski, Catherine Stonehouse, and Linda Cannell. *Children Matter: Celebrating Their Place in the Church, Family, and Community.* Grand Rapids, MI: William B. Eerdmans, 2005.

Miles, Glenn and Josephine-Joy Wright. *Celebrating Children.* Carlisle, Cumbria: Paternoster Press, 2003.

Miles, Glenn and Paul Stephenson. *Child Development Study Pack.* Teddington, UK: Tearfund, 1999.

Miles, Glenn and Paul Stephenson. *Children at Risk Guidelines.* Teddington, UK: Tearfund, 2000–2001. http://tilz.tearfund.org/Topics/Child+development/.

Myers, Glenn. *Children in Crisis.* Cumbria, UK: OM Publishing, 2006.

Panter-Brick, Catherine. "Street Children, Human Rights, and Public Health: A Critique and Future Directions." *Child, Youth and Environments* 13, No. 1 (Spring 2003): 147–171, http://www.colorado.edu/journals/cye/13_1/ Vol13_1Articles/panter-brick.pdf.

General Websites

Better Care Network: www.crin.org/bcn/
Children's Rights Information Network (CRIN): www.crin.org
Childwatch International: www.childwatch.uio.no
Celebrating Children Training: www.celebratingchildrentraining.info
Compassion International: www.compassion.com/default.htm
International Institute for Environment and Development: www.iied.org/pubs/
Plan International: www.plan-international.org/
Primary Years Program: www.ibo.org/pyp/index.cfm
Save the Children Sweden: www.rb.se
Tearfund: www.tearfund.org
United Nations Children's Fund (UNICEF): www.unicef.org
Viva: www.viva.org
Vulnerable Children Assistance Organization: www.vcao.org.kh/
World Vision International: www.wvi.org

Child Abuse, Exploitation, Trafficking, and Protection Books and Articles

Child Workers in Asia. "Our Voice, Our Values: Statements of the Children." Paper from the Child Forum against the Most Intolerable Forms of Child Labour, September 1–2, 1997. http://www.cwa.tnet.co.th/Voices/ref_voice3.html.

Delaney, Stephanie. *Protecting Children from Sexual Exploitation and Sexual Violence in Disaster and Emergency Situations.* Bangkok: ECPAT International, 2006. http://www.ecpat.net/EI/Publications/Care_Protection/Protecting_Children_from_CSEC_in%20Disaster_ENG.pdf.

Ennew, Judith, and Dominique Pierre Plateau. *How to Research the Physical and Emotional Punishment of Children.* Bangkok: Save the Children, 2004. http://www.dhr.go.cr/nopeguemos/pdf/how_to_research_the_physical_and_emotional_punishment.pdf.

Gelles, Richard J. and Jane B. Lancaster, eds. *Child Abuse and Neglect: Biosocial Dimensions.* New York: Aldine Transaction, 1987.

Lester, A. D., ed. *When Children Suffer: A Sourcebook for Ministry with Children in Crisis.* Philadelphia: The Westminster Press, 1987.

Oates, R. Kim. *The Spectrum of Child Abuse: Assessment, Treatment, and Prevention.* New York: Brunner/Mazel, Inc., 1996.

Panter-Brick, Catherine and Malcolm T. Smith. *Abandoned Children*. Cambridge, UK: Cambridge University Press, 2000.

UNICEF. "Violence against Children in East Asia and the Pacific Region." Summary of the East Asia and the Pacific Regional Consultation on the UN Study on Violence against Children, Bangkok, Thailand, June 14–16, 2005.

Child Abuse, Exploitation, Trafficking, and Protection Websites

Anti-slavery International: www.antislavery.org
Asha Forum: www.asha.viva.org
Child Workers in Asia: www.cwa.tnet.co.th
Chab Dai Coalition: www.chabdai.org
End Child Prostitution and Tourism (ECPAT): www.ecpat.net
Human Rights Watch: www.hrw.org
International Justice Mission: www.ijm.org
International Society for Prevention of Child Abuse and Neglect: www.ispcan.org
Keeping Children Safe: www.keepingchildrensafe.org.uk/
Love 146: www.love146.org

Child Participation Books and Articles

Boyden, Jo and Judith Ennew, eds. *Children in Focus: A Manual for Participatory Research with Children*. Stockholm, Sweden: Radda Barnen (Save the Children Sweden), 1997.

Brokaw, Meredith and Annie Gilbar. *The Penny Whistle Party Planner*. New York: Fireside, 1991.

Chambers, Robert. *Whose Reality Counts? Putting the First Last*. London: Intermediate Technology Publications Ltd., 1997.

Dorning, Karl and Tim O'Shaughnessy. "Creating Space for Children's Participation: Participatory Planning with Street Children in Yangon, Myanmar." Paper presented at the conference of the Australasian Evaluation Society, 2001. http://www.aes.asn.au/conferences/2001/refereed%20papers/Dorning%20-%20O'shaughnessy.pdf.

Fine, Gary Alan and Kent L. Sandstrom. *Knowing Children: Participant Observation with Minors*. Newbury Park: SAGE Publications, Inc., 1988.

Fraser, Sandy, ed. *Doing Research with Children and Young People*. London: SAGE Publications Ltd., The Open University, 2004.

Gibbs, Sara, Gillian Mann, and Nicola Mathers. *Child-to-Child: A Practical Guide: Empowering Children as Active Citizens.* London: Child-to-Child, 2002. http://www.child-to-child.org/guide/guide.pdf.

Greene, Sheila and Diane Hogan, eds. *Researching Children's Experience: Approaches and Methods.* London: SAGE Publications Ltd., 2005.

Greig, Anne, Jayne Taylor, and Thomas MacKay. *Doing Research with Children.* 2nd ed. London: SAGE Publications Ltd., 2007.

Inter-Agency Working Group on Children's Participation. *Children as Active Citizens: A Policy and Programme Guide: Commitments and Obligations for Children's Civil Rights and Civic Engagement in East Asia and the Pacific.* Bangkok: Inter-Agency Working Group on Children's Participation, 2008. http://www.iawgcp.com/download/Children_as_AC_A4_book.pdf.

———. *Children's Participation in Decision Making: Why Do It, When to Do It, How to Do It.* Bangkok: Inter-Agency Working Group on Children's Participation, 2007. http://www.iawgcp.com/download/wwh.pdf.

———. *Minimum Standards for Consulting with Children.* Bangkok: Inter-Agency Working Group on Children's Participation, 2007. http://www.iawgcp.com/download/ms.pdf.

———. *Operations Manual on Children's Participation in Consultations.* Bangkok: Inter-Agency Working Group on Children's Participation, 2007. http://www.iawgcp.com/download/om.pdf.

James, Allison and Pia Monrad Christensen, eds. *Research with Children: Perspectives and Practices.* London: Routledge, 2008.

Jayakaran, Ravi. *Facilitating Small Groups: A Resource Book.* Thailand: World Vision International—China, 2006.

———. *Participatory Process Assessment and Evaluation Manual.* Cambodia: MoEYS, DFID, and UNDP, 2006.

Johnson, Victoria, Joanna Hill, and Edda Ivan-Smith. *Listening to Smaller Voices: Children in an Environment of Change.* London: ActionAid, 1995.

Johnson, Victoria, Edda Ivan-Smith, Gill Gordon, Pat Pridmore, and Patta Scott. *Stepping Forward: Children and Young People's Participation in the Development Process.* London: Intermediate Technology Publications Ltd., 1998.

Kirby, Perpetua. *Involving Young Researchers: How to Enable Young People to Design and Conduct Research.* York, UK: York Publishing Services for Joseph Rowntree Foundation in association with Save the Children, 1999.

Kirby, Perpetua, Claire Lanyon, Kathleen Cronin, and Ruth Sinclair. *Building a Culture of Participation Involving Children and Young People in Policy, Service Planning, Delivery and Evaluation: Handbook.* London: DfES Publications, 2004.

Leadbeater, Bonnie, Elizabeth Banister, and Cecilia Benoit, eds. *Ethical Issues in Community-Based Research with Children and Youth.* Toronto: University of Toronto Press, 2006.

Lewis, Vicky, and Open University, eds. *The Reality of Research with Children and Young People.* London: SAGE Publications Ltd. in association with the Open University, 2004.

O'Kane, Claire. "Street and Working Children's Participation in Programming for their Rights." *Child, Youth and Environments* 13, No. 1 (Spring 2003): n.p., http://www.colorado.edu/journals/cye/13_1/Vol13ArticleReprints/Okane-forFinalVersion_Vol13(1).pdf.

Plan Asia Regional Office. *Children and the Tsunami: Engaging with Children in Disaster Response, Recovery and Risk Reduction: Learning from Children's Participation in the Tsunami Response.* Bangkok: Plan, 2005. http://www.planusa.org/stuff/contentmgr/files/d9ee355af9fc9e39564ba31f686d519b/miscdocs/int_children_tsunami.pdf.

Plan International. *Our Future; Our Say: Children Demand Action on the Millennium Development Goals.* Woking, Surrey, UK: Plan, 2005. http://www.plan-international.org/resources/publications/childrenmedia/ourfuture/.

Pretty, Jules N., Irene Guijt, John Thompson, and Ian Scoones. *Participatory Learning and Action: A Trainer's Guide.* London: IIED, 1995.

Ratna, K. and Reddy, N. *A Journey in Children's Participation.* Bangalore: The Concerned for Working Children, 2002.

Save the Children. *Child Participation: 12 Lessons Learned from Children's Participation in the UN General Assembly Special Session on Children.* London: Save the Children, 2004. http://www.savethechildren.net/alliance/resources/12lessons.pdf.

Save the Children Child Participation Working Group. *So You Want to Consult with Children? A Toolkit of Good Practice.* London: International Save the Children Alliance, 2003. http://www.savethechildren.net/alliance/resources/childconsult_toolkit_final.pdf.

Shephard, Carol. *Participation: Spice It Up! Practical Tools for Engaging Children and Young People in Planning and Consultations.* London: Save the Children, 2002.

Child Participation Websites

Better Care Network: www.crin.org/bcn/
The Free Child Project: www.freechild.org/ladder.htm
Informal Working Group on Participatory Approaches and Methods: http://www.fao.org/Participation/
Inter-Agency Working Group on Children's Participation: http://www.iawgcp.com/
Knowing Children: www.knowingchildren.org
Plan International: www.plan-international.org/
Save the Children Sweden: www.rb.se
Tearfund: www.tearfund.org
World Vision International: www.wvi.org

* * *

GLOSSARY AND ABBREVIATIONS

Acquired Immune Deficiency Syndrome (AIDS): AIDS is the late stage of Human Immunodeficiency Virus (HIV) infection, when a person's immune system is severely damaged and has difficulty fighting diseases and certain cancers.

Advocacy: The process by which we take up an issue and get support for it by way of intervention from those in authority.

Blessing Analysis: An exercise that helps assess blessings.

Capacity/Vulnerability Analysis: A process by which the capacity and vulnerability of a person, group, village or strategy is assessed. It is similar to a SWOT (Strengths, Weaknesses, Opportunities and Threats) analysis, with the difference that capacities involve the "strengths and opportunities" and vulnerabilities include the "weaknesses and threats." The analysis helps determine dimensions that need improvement or correction

Causal Diagram of Disease: A way to determine the causes of disease in a community using the community or group perspective.

Child Abuse: The circumstance under which a child's rights are denied. It could be by acts of omission or commission. There is a whole range of issues (depending on intensity) that can be classified as child abuse.

Child Domestic Worker (CDW): The practice of having a child (defined as a person below the age of sixteen years) who is often a 'live-in' member with the family and works full time carrying out domestic work for the family. These arrangements are often extremely exploitative.

Child-centered: A program where activities are often carried out in a way that is "paternalistic," with direct benefits for the child; for example, the provision of school uniforms, school supplies, food, shelter, etc.

Child-focused: When a program is so focused that the final outcome of the combination of activities is designed to make an impact on improving the child's well-being. For instance, the digging of a well is designed to ensure that the child has access to safe drinking water.

Child Participation: Occurs when the child is involved in the needs assessment, designing, planning, implementing, and evaluation of a program.

Child Protection: Action taken to ensure a child is kept safe from harm physically, mentally, socially, emotionally, and spiritually.

Community: A group of people that live in socio-economic interaction with each other and in close proximity, who identify themselves as belonging to the same group. They may be those of similar ethnicity, similar financial status, similar belief, or who live in close proximity to each other.

Community Development: The process by which we work with a community to develop it and enable it to develop and grow its survival strategy.

Children's Participation Plan: A plan that has been developed by the children who will benefit from it.

Culture: The combination of practices that a community follows that uniquely represent their ethnicity or uniqueness.

Deprivation-Exclusion-Vulnerability Index (DEV Index): A tool to determine the level of risk that children in a community face.

Focus Group: A small group that represents the members of the larger community. This is the group that you will work with to find out about their community.

Focused Group Discussion (FGD): A conversation between members of the focus group that has specific goals and outcomes.

Holistic Worldview Analysis (HWVA): A method used to understand worldview.

Household Food Security Status (HHFSS): A tool to categorize a household based on how many months out of the year they are able to meet their household's food needs. This tool is also referred to as the RFSA or Rapid (Household) Food Security Status Assessment.

Human Immunodeficiency Virus (HIV): The virus that can lead to Acquired Immune Deficiency Syndrome (AIDS). HIV damages a person's body by destroying specific blood cells, called CD4+T cells, which are crucial to helping the body fight diseases.

Independence Assessment: The means by which we assess the degree of independence a child has in various dimensions of his or her life, especially with reference to deciding his or her future.

Macro: The profile of a situation at the macro-level, namely at the district, province, state, or country level.

Macro Zoom PLA: A participatory learning and action exercise conducted at the broader macro level to understand an issue.

Matrix: A grid with columns going up and down and rows going left and right; useful for ranking the importance of each category.

Non-Governmental Organization (NGO): Often, organizations working within the community for the community's benefit.

Participatory Learning and Action (PLA): A method used to facilitate community participation in research.

Participatory Rural Appraisal (PRA): A method used to facilitate community participation in research among rural communities.

Personal Empowerment Assessment: A way of assessing how empowered an individual is in making decisions or taking action with reference to their future.

Principles: The set of agreed upon guidelines or actions on the basis of which one deals with children. When one follows a series of given principles the outcome can usually be predicted.

Problem Analysis: The means by which one analyzes the problems that children encounter in their daily life.

Rapid Holistic Health Assessment (RHHA): The means by which one assesses what factors lead to a child's well being and holistic health.

Rapport: The trust and support that must be developed before members of a community will share important information with you.

Self-esteem: The factors that determine what makes a child see himself or herself as being of value and significance to their peers and elders.

Self-worth: The factors that determine what makes a child see himself or herself as being of value and significance to their peers and elders.

Strategy: The predetermined series of plans of action that one adopts to achieve one's long-term goals.

Survival Strategy: The survival strategy of an individual or a community is defined as the strategy that they adopt to survive and keep life going.

Ten-Seed Technique (TST): A tool used to determine proportions.

Trends Analysis: An analysis of events to see if they conform to some clearly emerging patterns showing the futuristic direction of events.

Triangulation: The process of seeking other perspectives to ensure that information is not biased or one-sided.

Uncertainty Analysis: An analysis of events to see if there are events that though they are problems, do not always occur on a yearly cycle, though they may have the potential of happening at anytime.

Worldview: The worldview of an individual or a community is the lens or framework by which they perceive their world. Analyzing this enables one to understand the individual or community's survival strategy and thus its capacities and vulnerabilities. Once this is done it is possible to develop an intervention.

* * *

BIBLIOGRAPHY

Ashley, Holly, Nicole Kenton, and Angela Milligan, eds. *Participatory Learning and Action 56*. London: International Institute for Environment and Development, 2007.

Chambers, Robert. *Participatory Workshops: A Sourcebook of 21 Sets of Ideas and Activities*. London: Earthscan, 2002.

Chambers, Robert, Nicole Kenton, and Holly Ashley, eds. *Participatory Learning and Action 50*. London: International Institute for Environment and Development, 2004.

Charoensuk, Dusadee. "Needs, Self-esteem and Health Impact Assessment of Orphans Due to AIDS in Thailand." Presentation at the international conference, "Sustainable Development for Peace: New Dimensions of Friendly Cooperation in the Upper Mekong Sub-region," Phnom Penh, Kingdom of Cambodia, September 25–28, 2006.

"Child Neglect." *Psychology Today*. http://psychologytoday.com/conditions/childneglect.html (accessed August 20, 2008).

Forbes, Bill. *Celebrating Children Training Series #6: Child Protection* (working title). Edited by Glenn Miles, Jennifer Orona, and Miriam Packard. Forthcoming, 2009.

Gandhi, Mahatma. "Mahatma Gandhi." http://www.cybernation.com/victory/quotations/authors/quotes_gandhi_mahatma.html (accessed January 12, 2009).

Global Forum for Child Survival, Atlanta, GA, Carter Center, 1996.

Gordon, Graham. *Understanding Advocacy*. Teddington, UK: Tearfund, 2002. http://tilz.tearfund.org/webdocs/Tilz/Roots/English/Advocacy%20toolkit/Advocacy%20toolkit_E_FULL%20DOC_Parts%20A%2BB.pdf.

Hart, Roger. *Children's Participation: From Tokenism to Citizenship*. Florence: UNICEF Innocenti Research Centre, 1992.

Howard-Grabman, Lisa and Gail Snetro. *How to Mobilize Communities for Health and Social Change*. Health Communication Partnership, 2006. http://www.savethechildren.org/publications/.

Jayakaran, Ravi. *Participatory Poverty Alleviation and Development.* Khon Kaen, Thailand: World Vision International—China, 2003. Also available as a CD-ROM from www.map.org.

———. "The Ten Seed Technique: Learning How the Community Sees Itself." *Child Survival Connections* (Spring 2002). http://www.childsurvival.com/connections/Connections_Spring%202002.pdf.

———. "TST—Ten Seed Technique." http://www.fao.org/Participation/ft_show.jsp?ID=1981.

Jayakaran, Ravi et al. "Studies of Food Security-Related Vulnerability." World Vision Asia Pacific Region, 2001.

Keeping Children Safe. http://www.keepingchildrensafe.org.uk/.

Kilbourn, Phyllis, ed. *Shaping the Future: Girls and Our Destiny.* Pasadena, CA: William Carey Library, 2008.

McConnell, Douglas, Jennifer Orona, and Paul Stockley, eds. *Understanding God's Heart for Children: Toward a Biblical Framework.* Colorado Springs: Authentic, 2007.

Mulan. DVD and VHS. Directed by Tony Bancroft and Barry Cook. Orlando, FL: Walt Disney Feature Animation, 1998.

Neimann, Sandy, Devorah Greenstein, and Darlena David. *Helping Children Who Are Deaf: Family and Community Support for Children Who Do Not Hear Well.* Berkeley, CA: Hesperian Foundation, 2004.

Niemann, Sandy and Namita Jacob. *Helping Children Who Are Blind: Family and Community Support for Children with Vision Problems.* Berkeley, CA: Hesperian Foundation, 2000.

O'Grady, Ron. *The Child and the Tourist: The Story Behind the Escalation of Child Prostitution in Asia.* Auckland, New Zealand: ECPAT, 1992.

Save the Children. *Learning to Listen: Consulting Children and Young People with Disabilities.* London: Save the Children, n.d. http://www.childinfo.org/files/childdisability_SavetheChildren.pdf.

———. *Practice Standards in Child Participation.* London: Save the Children, n.d. http://www.savethechildren.net/alliance/about_us/accountability/practicestandardscp.doc.

Stephenson, Paul, with Steve Gourley and Glenn Miles. *Child Participation.* Teddington, UK: Tearfund, 2004. http://tilz.tearfund.org/Publications/ROOTS/Child+participation.htm.

UNICEF. "Female Genital Mutilation/Cutting." http://www.unicef.org/protection/index_genitalmutilation.html (accessed February 11, 2009).

———. *State of the World's Children 2003: Child Participation.* Geneva: UNICEF, 2002.

United Nations. *Convention on the Rights of the Child*. Geneva: United Nations, 1989. http://www2.ohchr.org/english/law/crc.htm.

Werner, David. *Disabled Village Children: A Guide for Community Health Workers, Rehabilitation Workers, and Families*. Berkeley, CA: Hesperian Foundation, 2006.

* * *

Index

minority people groups, 33, 215
mobilization
    of support, 4-5
modernization, 37-38
Myanmar, 63

N
negligence, neglect, 31-32, 34, 185-86
    impact of prior, 31
Non-Governmental Organization (NGO), 33, 43, 62, 93, 97, 114, 122, 145, 151, 160, 167-68, 186, 188-91, 195-96, 206-08, 211-13, 223-27, 234
        staff, 97, 160, 173, 212, 224
nutrition, 60, 101, 186
    improvement programs, 169
    nutritional value, 101

O
O'Grady, Ron, 185
opportunity, 3, 8, 28, 30, 33, 35, 56, 77, 139, 165, 191
orphan, 32, 48, 128

P
Participatory Learning and Action (PLA), 54, 69, 229
Participatory Poverty Alleviation and Development, 53
Participatory Rural Appraisal (PRA), 54
patience, 37, 40, 68, 154, 226
peace, 153-54
perception, 38, 40, 51, 72-73, 99, 111, 143-45, 148, 151, 220, 229-31
perseverance, 40
personal empowerment assessment, 113
play
        dramatic play, 45
        in a child's life. *See* children.
        learning and development, 44
        pretending, 44
politician, 35
poverty, 20-25, 27-28, 30-31, 34, 165, 172, 189-90, 215
        as violence, 22, 27
        excruciating, 22, 27

CPSIA information can be obtained
at www.ICGtesting.com
Printed in the USA
BVHW031224210922
647645BV00007B/130

9 780878 080014